# Gardening in Containers

*By the Editors of Sunset Magazine
and Sunset Books*

Lane Books · Menlo Park, California

ON THE COVER: The *Sunset* patio in early spring glows with the bright blossoms of plants in containers. In the foreground are pink hyacinths, lavender crocus, and stately daffodils in clay pots. Wooden boxes on the left hold an azalea and a reticulata camellia. Contorted plant in wooden box at right is Medusa's head euphorbia *(Euphorbia caput-medusae)*. Photograph by Robert Cox.

Fourth Printing February 1969

*All rights reserved throughout the world*
*Copyright © 1967 by Lane Magazine & Book Company,*
*Menlo Park, California*
*Second Edition*
*Library of Congress Catalog Card: 67-24382*
*Title Number 320*
*Lithographed in the U.S.A.*

# CONTENTS

# WHAT IS CONTAINER GARDENING?

Why grow plants in containers? • Fundamentals of container gardening
More work or less? • Containers—kinds to
choose from, some to make

The popularity of raising plants in containers has accelerated in recent years, but it has been a favorite gardening practice for centuries. From the time some unrecorded man admired a prehistoric bloom and brought it in a clump of earth to his dwelling through the periods of pot culture developed by the Egyptians, Romans, and Orientals, there has been a unique delight in singling out, displaying, and being responsible for special plants that particularly interest us.

Container gardening is adaptable and versatile. Almost any plant can be grown — at least for a time — in a box or pot. Most can be moved indoors for short periods. In fact, gardening in containers allows latitude for experimentation with plants that your local climate might forbid. To a limited degree, you can *create* a climate for a container-grown plant merely by changing its position in the garden or house.

Pot gardening not only makes it possible to have plants you couldn't otherwise grow, it gives you a chance to try out new ones — one at a time or in groups. You can water, feed, and care for a potted plant and if you don't like it or it doesn't agree with the location you have provided, it can be moved away without leaving a gaping hole in the garden.

A plant may go unnoticed when massed with other plants, but when it is isolated in a container in a special setting it takes on a definite personality. Some plants, Japanese maple and various kinds of azaleas for instance, have particular characteristics — growth structure, flowers, or foliage — that make them natural container subjects.

It is almost impossible for container gardening to be monotonous. Plants can be kept on the move. The best each season has to offer can be brought on-stage for maximum display and then taken off-stage when the peak show is past.

## What to expect from this book

The following chapters not only give lists of plants particularly suited to container life as well as directions for their care but also show examples of a variety of containers and suggest places to use them.

On the following page is a list of the fundamentals of container gardening. Particulars are discussed in other chapters.

*A CONTAINER GARDEN brings the fresh look of spring up close where every bloom can be enjoyed as it opens. Daffodils are flanked with ferns, azaleas, grape hyacinths, and bonsai.*

## FUNDAMENTALS OF CONTAINER GARDENING

Here is a checklist of basic points to be observed in container gardening. Detailed information is given in the following chapters.

**CONTAINERS** • Select a container of the right size and shape for the growth characteristics and appearance of your plant.

**SOIL MIX** • Generally, container plants do best in a porous, fast-draining mix with added nutrients.

**WATERING** • Most experts consider regular watering the most important factor in container gardening. Plants restricted in space need more frequent watering than their counterparts planted in open ground.

**DRAINAGE** • Most plants need the rapid drainage provided by a porous potting mix. Few plants can survive in a heavy or clay soil in a container.

**FEEDING** • Generally, plants grown in pots and boxes should be fed regularly during the active growing season. With heavy watering, nutrients leach readily through porous soil mixes.

**LOCATION** • Because roots on container-grown plants are exposed to high and low temperatures (through the walls of the container), they are more sensitive to extremes than those in open ground. Move tender plants into protected locations in winter.

**REPOTTING** • Most plants need repotting in fresh soil mix when their roots fill the container. Generally, move the plant on to the next size pot. If it is an older, slow-growing plant, shave off 1 or 2 inches from the outside of the root ball and replant in the same container with fresh mix. Some plants, such as agapanthus, bloom better when slightly rootbound.

**PEST CONTROL** • The same pests and diseases that attack plants in the garden also prey on those in pots. Diseased plants in boxes and tubs can be isolated for treatment, thus avoiding the spread of infection or infestation.

**INDOOR PLANTS** • Many plants can be rotated between outdoors and indoors for short periods. (See the next chapter for culture of indoor-outdoor plants, house plants, and bonsai; also page 59, 66.)

## MORE WORK OR LESS?

Although most container-grown plants require more frequent watering and feeding than those in the ground, there are compensations for extra effort and ways in which you can reduce maintenance.

When soil is too water-logged and heavy for early-spring planting, you can still have color from flowering plants started earlier in pots in a protected spot.

Group containers to cut down on time and effort in watering, especially during vacations. Remove spent blooms and yellowed or damaged leaves at the same time. Or cart away any unsightly plant to an out-of-the-way spot and spruce it up when you have time.

A word of caution: Don't underestimate the weight of a soil-filled container. When planted, a box 1 foot square and 1 foot high can weigh from 50 to 90 pounds. Use mechanical aids, such as casters, handtrucks, or rollers to move containers efficiently. See page 33.

*EASY TO CARRY off-stage when white violas fade, these stained redwood boxes can be filled with sun-loving dwarf zinnias, other summer annuals.*

*PLANTED TO STAY in one shady spot, a fluted concrete container is an elegant and appropriate setting for dark green Tasmanian tree fern.*

## CONTAINERS ARE HALF THE PICTURE

In container gardening, the container is half the picture. And a handsome plant deserves a handsome planter. The container, by definition, can be anything in which a plant will grow — from an antique Chinese brass urn to a terra cotta pot, a clay flue tile, a wooden box, or even a crevice in a piece of volcanic rock. Boxes and pots also are made of plastic, metal, and a variety of synthetic materials.

### Requirements of a good container

Ideally, a container is expected to hold up well against the intermittent watering and drying out which cause decay. It should hold moisture long enough to satisfy the plant, yet drain readily. Cleats under wood boxes and feet on clay pots permit free drainage and increase air circulation, thus helping to prevent decay in certain kinds of wood and to discourage harboring pests.

Provide saucers or trays under indoor containers or those standing on outdoor patios or decks that stain. To prevent seepage through saucers of clay or other porous materials, coat the inside with an asphalt or other waterproof paint.

### Where to buy

You'll have little trouble finding a container. They are available everywhere from nurseries to dime stores and art galleries. Costs vary from inexpensive unglazed pots to handmade, one-of-a-kind containers that carry a substantial price tag. But in situations where the container also serves as a decorative feature — a piece of art — you'll find the high cost justified. If you do buy one of a special design or color, it is a good idea to take it along when you shop for a plant to put in it.

### Making your own

Sometimes it is easier to make your own container in order to get just the right size and shape for the place you want to put it. Rot-resistant woods such as cedar and redwood are the most popular building material for planters, but they also can be made of metal, concrete, or clay. See pages 12-17 for directions on constructing containers.

### Container size and shape

Select a container adapted to the size and shape of the plant you want to grow. The container's appearance — color, shape, texture — should not detract from the good looks of the living plant. Compatible plants and container suggestions are discussed in chapter 3. Containers that are generally available are shown on the following pages.

*WHITE PORCELAIN POT intensifies the effect of pure white bloom of azalea 'Albion' in cool shade with other azaleas, evergreens.*

COLLECTION OF CONTAINERS is a sampling of many types available: *1, 2,* and *3. Hexagonal tubs, 18-inch diameter, 14-inch,* and *12-inch. 4. Concrete bowl with 30-inch diameter. 5. White glazed terra cotta pot. 6. Soy tub, 14-inch diameter. 7, 8,* and *9. Redwood boxes with a variety of finishes. 10. Clay hanging pot, 13½-inch diameter, 7 inches deep.*

*11. Standard pot and saucer, 12-inch. 12. Standard fern pot (also called azalea pot and ¾ type pot), 8-inch. 13. Flare-sided redwood box, 22 by 17 inches. 14. Strawberry jar, 12-inch diameter. 15. Mexican terra cotta olla. 16, 17,* and *18. Glazed brown clay bonsai pots. 19. Redwood box, 35 by 9 inches. 20, 21. 3-legged clay pots, 9-inch and 11-inch.*

DRILL DRAIN HOLES in concrete bowls with a star drill. Tap lightly with a hammer as drill is slowly rotated. Water in bowl makes job easier.

## Clay pots — the near-perfect containers

Common clay flowerpots come close to being ideal plant containers. They are available nearly everywhere, come in many sizes and a variety of shapes, and are relatively inexpensive. Pots look attractive in most situations and on most surfaces. Potted plants can be plunged into garden beds for a time and then cleaned up and placed on a deck for display. Potted bulbs can be buried in peat moss, wood shavings, or sawdust until roots form and top growth starts. The main disadvantages of porous clay pots is that they are breakable and they dry out quite rapidly, especially in warm weather.

The earthy colors of unglazed terra cotta pots blend with *anything* you care to put in them. Clay pots come in the familiar brick red, yellowish tan, off-white, and chocolate brown (the usual color of the unglazed classic bonsai pot).

Unglazed pots still outsell glazed ones after hundreds of years of popularity. Glazed pots have non-porous surfaces so do not need as frequent watering. Glazed pots, sold in white, black, and a variety of colors, can contribute a bright note to a living room or patio — *if the color is chosen wisely*. Be sure that the pot color doesn't clash with the flowers or foliage of the plant.

A wide variety of sizes and shapes of terra cotta pots is sold, although few if any nurseries carry all types. In most areas there is at least one nursery, garden supply shop, or florist that specializes in containers. If there is a pottery manufacturing plant in your vicinity, learn whether it would be possible to visit and see a much wider selection than is found in the average retail outlet.

Clay pot sizes are defined by their diameter measurements. Although proportions vary somewhat from one manufacturer to another, these are the most useful and popular kinds of pots:

**STANDARD** • Traditional favorites, these pots are at least as tall as they are wide across the top and frequently are taller. They have heavy, wide rims and are made in 2-inch to 16-inch sizes.

Developed primarily for propagation in the florist and nursery trade in the days when nursery stock was sold in clay pots instead of cans and plastic bands, their proportion is more utilitarian than beautiful. Although greater depth provides more root space, the pot often seems too tall for the plant.

**STANDARD FERN POTS (ALSO CALLED AZALEA POTS, 3/4 POTS)** • Three-quarters as high as wide, these pots are in better proportion to most plants than the regular standard. They are excellent for plants, such as azaleas, with shallow root systems and are available in 4-inch to 14-inch sizes.

**VENETIAN POTS** • Slightly in-curving at the top, the sides are ringed with a design of concentric bands impressed into the clay. Symmetrical and somewhat formal, Venetian pots come in 7½-inch to 20-inch sizes.

**SPANISH POTS** • Graceful pots with outward sloping sides and slightly flaring lips, they are made in 8-inch to 12-inch sizes. Spanish fern pots from 12 to 18 inches are made also.

**PANS** • Bulb pans, or seed pans, vary slightly but usually are less than half as high as wide. They resemble deep pot saucers, but have drain holes. Six-inch to 12-inch sizes are available.

**CLAY BOWLS** • A variety of bowl-shaped planters is made. Some are shallow, wide, and round-bottomed. Others have feet; and some have widely flaring sides. In specialty shops, unusual shapes like the strawberry jar and Mexican *olla* can often be found.

Concrete and aggregate containers are becoming increasingly popular. Because the material is restricted only by the mold into which it is poured, there are many styles, usually in large sizes.

*VENETIAN POT with its simple design of concentric rings enhances the naturally pendulous branches, pink blooms of* Camellia saluenensis *'J. C. Williams.'*

*GRACEFULLY FLARED Spanish pot heightens the effect of golden shrub daisy (Euryops pectinatus); bright yellow flowers and gray leaves.*

*TRIO OF REDWOOD BOXES displays gray-green* Podocarpus gracilior *in lightly shaded entry court. Plants are staked and tops secured to eaves.*

*BLACK-PAINTED HALF BARREL, 26 inches wide and 18 inches deep, holds Japanese black pine, pruned to reveal branch structure.*

## Boxes, Tubs, and Barrels

Husky wooden boxes, tubs, and barrels are the garden workhorses. They are suited to any job from holding an outsized tree to housing a portable collection of annuals.

Roughly defined, the difference between a box and a tub is the basic shape. A box is usually rectangular while a tub has a circular or hexagonal base and is traditionally constructed of staves held in place by hoops. Barrels, soy tubs, and kegs fit this description, but also the large round ceramic containers often are referred to as tubs.

The high insulating value of wood insures that heat from even the hot summer sun will penetrate slowly, thus protecting the plant roots from drying and scorching. Redwood and cedar both fit the decay-resisting, moisture holding, and insulating requirements of a good container. In some areas, cypress, black locust, osage orange, or chestnut boxes may be available. None of these woods really requires a preservative treatment. But if you wish, coat the inside with a preservative paint or asphalt compound, or fit in a liner made of a cut-down 5-gallon can with holes punched in the bottom.

All tubs and boxes should be designed so that the joints will remain tight to prevent excess moisture loss. Holes should be provided in the bottom to facilitate drainage. The bottom of the tub should not rest directly on the ground but should be raised an inch or more with legs, blocks, or cleats.

Let the expected shape of the plant at maturity determine the shape of the box you choose. A square box is appropriate for a low, bushy gardenia, azalea, or dwarf citrus. A tall tub fits a tapering false cypress or boxwood. And a three-quarter height barrel is suitable for a handsome Japanese maple.

Remember that plant boxes and tubs must be deep enough to allow sufficient root growth. Lantana, azalea, gardenia, and bouvardia require 12 to 18 inches. Camellia, rhododendron, kumquat, and viburnum need from 18 to 24 inches.

Consider the weight problem if you plan on moving your tubs or boxes. Because a cubic foot of soil weighs from 50 to 90 pounds, a 2-by-2-foot box can mount up to hundreds of pounds.

**BARRELS** • Try to obtain barrels which have been built to hold liquids. These have thicker walls and are less apt to leak. Coating the inside with wood preservative and the hoops with rust deterrent will lengthen the barrel's lifetime.

The weakest point in barrel construction is the joint where the bottom fits into the staves. Do not support the full weight on the rim (or staves) of the barrel. To the bottom attach a cleat that is thick enough to raise the rim of the barrel slightly above ground level so that the weight is borne by the bottom, not the rim.

**WINDOW BOXES** • Window boxes usually are large containers and, when planted, become a very heavy load to hang on the side of any house. Prime considerations should be: secure supports (lag screws or bolts) to anchor the box to the house studs, at least 1-inch lumber to prevent the box from warping, seams calked to prevent drainage stains on the house. Boxes should have at least a 9-inch depth for most root systems.

*WINDOW BOX VARIATION is shelf made with circular holes large enough to hold pots. Colorful begonias, annuals can be replaced with evergreen ivy.*

*SHOWERS OF WHITE STARS of campanula nearly hide container. Wood hanging baskets are favored in warm areas as wood holds moisture well.*

## Hanging containers

A hanging container really spotlights a plant, bringing it right up to eye level, giving a garden a luxuriant and well-furnished look.

Although hanging baskets and pots actually are intended for trailing plants, usually sedate plants such as camellia or azalea can become quite acrobatic with their branches curving downward like picture hooks. Fuchsias, petunias, campanulas, and trailing geraniums are long-time favorites. Less used but choice are shrimp plant and bush morning glory. Herbs and cherry tomatoes are attractive and practical.

Several kinds are available: terra cotta pots, decorative ceramic pots, redwood or cedar boxes, or moss-lined wire baskets.

In a cool summer climate, plants will thrive in any kind of a container. But if you live in a warmer inland section, wooden boxes which soak up and hold the moisture longer are a better choice than clay pots; the latter evaporate much water from their surfaces and take about twice as much watering.

Suspend containers from substantial lag-thread clothesline hooks or screweyes. These are strong enough to bear the weight of the basket and not pull out. Use strong galvanized wire for hanging containers from hooks.

The drip and overflow from plants that hang above a patio can create a waterstain problem. Some gardeners use a single pot with a water-holding saucer attached below. See photo at right. Wrought iron plant holders with built-in drip pans are useful also.

See page 56 for a list of hanging plants.

*CAKE PANS, suspended by small chains, keep water from dripping and staining patio. Clay pots contain fuchsias, ivy geranium (foreground).*

## CONTAINERS YOU CAN MAKE

Often the only way to get a box just the shape, size, and appearance that you want for a particular spot is to build your own. Frequently you can convert an article intended for some other use — a flue tile or a Chinese *wok* — into a handsome and unique planter. But, generally, the most popular and versatile building material is wood.

### Wood and how to use it

Durable and easy to build, wood containers will resist decay longer if you take a few extra steps. Treat the joints with white lead or linseed oil. Glue and screw the corners. Paint the inside and bottom of the container with a wood preservative such as pentachlorophenol or waterproof it with an inside coating of asphalt paint or tree seal. Or, line the box with plastic sheeting, stapled to fit snugly. Finish with a wood stain or a beeswax finish, or leave the wood in its natural condition. Metal stains from nails or screws can be avoided by joining seams with dowels.

**REDWOOD AND CEDAR** • Both are widely used because they resist decay and age beautifully with little or no outside finish.

**DOUGLAS FIR** • It is stronger than redwood or cedar, an advantage for large boxes. When treated with a preservative, it will last many years. Stain the outside to keep it from turning dark.

**PINE** • Soft and easy to work, it should be treated with a preservative.

**EXTERIOR PLYWOOD** • It is both light weight and very strong. Careful construction is needed as all edges, joints and inside surfaces should be sealed as the container is built. Cover the top raw edge with a cap.

### Start with a simple box

Use hand tools to put together a basic box (12 by 14 by 14 inches) of rough redwood or cedar and you'll have a simple container that flatters nearly any plant. Or, you can do all sorts of things to vary and accent the design.

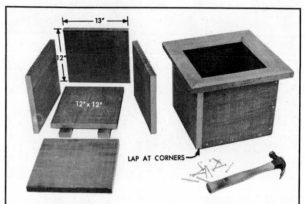

*MATERIALS: five pieces 1 by 12 lumber; 1 by 3 surfaced stock for cap; 1 by 1 cleats for feet; 12-penny nails.*

*VARY DESIGN with aluminum angle strips at corners. Or, nail ½ by 1-inch lath vertically around box.*

*SHINGLES CLOAK outside of basic planter, which is made of exterior plywood. Shingles match weathered stain finish on the house.*

*MIDWAY RAIL of 2 by 5 lumber varies boxes' basic design. Made of 2 by 12 redwood, planters were designed by Kathryn Stedman.*

## Big plants need big boxes

The big container plays a special role in the garden. Usually it houses a star performer — either a striking shrub, a small tree, or a mass of annuals to give seasonal color to a new garden.

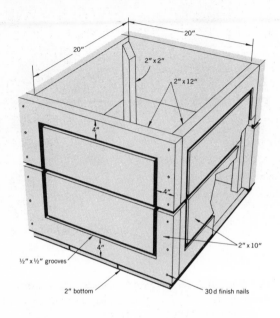

BUILD A BIG CONTAINER of 2-inch redwood. Overlap two sides. Nail on 2-inch thick bottom and seal joints with emulsified asphalt.

HOLD SIDES together by nailing 2 by 2's at inside corners. Dado or rout rectangular design and joint between 2 by 10's of each side.

## Small boxes for small plants

Combed wood boxes enhance the beauty of small plants. Build a simple box of 1-inch rough redwood, butting the sides and fastening with dowels instead of nails. The bottom and feet can be nailed on. To bring out the grain, burn the redwood with a blowtorch and remove the charred wood with a wire brush.

BLOWTORCH BURNS out soft portions of the wood but doesn't effect the hard grain. Don't burn inside of the box, as soil will cover.

WIRE BRUSH removes charred parts. Lumber also may be charred before box is built. For waxy finish, use mixture of turpentine, beeswax, linseed oil.

## Two take-apart boxes

Take-apart boxes are for big plants you want to take out, root prune and replant in the same box. In both boxes shown here one or more sides come off, facilitating the plant's removal.

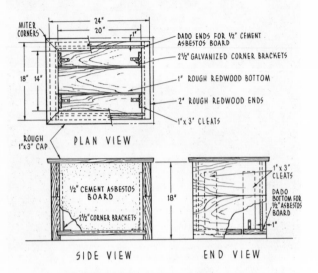

*CAP LIFTS and asbestos board sides pull out of grooves in ends. Container requires only dado cuts in sides, bottom; miter cuts for cap.*

*CONVENIENT REMOVAL of sides facilitates root pruning of Aleppo pine. Box is easy to build; wooden ends are wire-brushed for texture.*

Initial cost of the custom-made box below is high due to the hardware used, but it is worth it in terms of long service and convenience.

Build a base of two layers of 2-inch rough redwood. Construct two sides, the bottoms of which are the same width as the base. On the inside of these two sides attach cleats 4 inches in from the vertical edges. Bore three ½-inch holes 1½ inches in from each vertical edge. The other two sides are 6 inches narrower than the base.

Place the wide sides inside cleats nailed to the base; hold with screws through base cleat into side. Position the two narrow sides, butting ends against inside of wide sides. Hold narrow sides in place with six ½-inch tie rods strung through holes in wide sides and secured with washers and nuts.

*KNOCKDOWN, gray-stained box is big—34 inches square at top, 27 inches at bottom, and 20 inches deep inside. Bottom fitted with casters.*

*EVERY TWO OR THREE YEARS, Meyer lemon root ball is shaved with sharp spade, new soil mix added. Repot in cool weather while somewhat dormant.*

## Flare-sided container

A complete garden in miniature can be grown in this flare-sided box. A base and beveled top give it an attractive finish. The box is heavy, so it is best planted where it will remain.

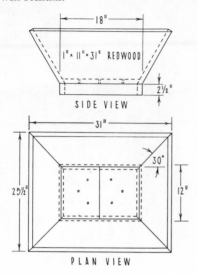

*RECTANGULAR BOX is constructed of one-inch cedar. Mitered corners, beveled top give box a well-made appearance. Attach heavy base.*

*MINIATURE GARDEN includes primroses, nandina, but bulbs in spring or annuals in summer would make an attractive box garden.*

## Sculptured trough

This handsome redwood planter is really an imitation clay hog trough. After the glued sides have set overnight, sculpture them with a disk sander to achieve the undulating lines.

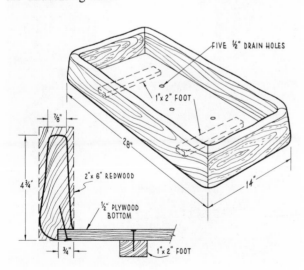

*MAKE A PICTURE FRAME of 2 by 6 redwood. Rabbet lower edge to fit in bottom. Miter corners, glue with waterproof glue, let set overnight.*

*APPLY UNEQUAL PRESSURE with sander to achieve undulating outlines of trough. Or remove wood with chisel or router; nail bottom in place.*

## Six more container ideas

Often you can create a dramatic new container just by re-working an old plain one or by using items not really meant for plants at all — such as a metal tank end, a plow disk, or even a cement block.

*1. VACATION FIND, this log provides natural environment for ferns, succulents. Scooped-out log garden is about 8 by 30 inches.*

*2. CLAY PIPE CYLINDER, natural colored and rough textured, holds bougainvillea. Bracket is curved, welded reinforcing iron.*

*3. COPPER BOXES flatter plants but often are costly. This one isn't—it is an old box covered with 25-cents-a-foot copper sheathing.*

*CUT COPPER with scissors, making each side separately. Leave a little extra to fold under, and tack down with copper tacks.*

4. *TRANSFORM FLATS* of annuals into temporary planters before placing plants in ground. Use brick collar to hide the flat.

5. *TALLER COLLAR* of 1 by 8 lumber holds flat of petunias at normal planter height. Finish with washable exterior paint. Collars stack neatly.

*NURSERY FLAT* rests on short 1 by 2 legs in corners of tall collar. Build collar to fit loosely as flats vary in size.

6. *PORTABLE ESPALIER* and bisque clay pot are simple in design and ideally suit symmetry of a two-year-old sasanqua camellia.

# HOW TO GARDEN IN CONTAINERS

Preparing the container • Potting the plant • Soil mixes • How to water
Feeding container plants • Pest and disease control • Pruning and
training • Weather protection • How to move big containers
Propagation • Care of house plants,
indoor-outdoor plants, bonsai

Even if you buy a plant already set in an attractive container, sometime it will have to be removed and placed in the next size pot, or root-pruned and returned to the same container. And here begins your first responsibility to the plant: Put it in a clean container that is the right size, give it a satisfactory soil mix, and transplant it again when its roots have filled the available space (unless it is one of those plants that seem to bloom best when pot-bound, such as agapanthus).

## PREPARING THE CONTAINER

Prepare a container before you move a plant into it. Take the trouble to scrub it well, as dirty pots and boxes may harbor insect eggs and fungus spores, troubles you don't want to pass on to the new occupants. Use a scraper or a stiff brush and water.

Before you use a container — old or new — soak it well. The countless tiny pores in the pot or box should be filled with water so they will not absorb moisture from the root ball of the plant, causing it to shrink away from the sides of the container. If this happens, water from later irrigations will drain around the root ball without wetting it.

*BEFORE TRANSPLANTING yellow 'Girl Scout' roses from nursery cans to containers, this gardener cut flowers for arrangements. The cutting induces new growth and more bloom.*

Each drain hole in the container should be covered with a curved piece of broken pot or a small square of screening. Do *not* put a layer of rock or gravel in the bottom of the pot. This old-time practice has been discredited by soil scientists.

Water is held by surface tension on the faces of soil particles — the finer the soil particles, the more total surface there is to hold the water. Penetration is best when soil texture is homogeneous throughout the root area.

## PUTTING PLANTS IN POTS

After the drain holes have been covered with pottery or screen to hold in the soil, put in a cushion of potting mix (see soil chart, page 20). The mix should be damp but not soggy. Set the plant on this layer and fill in around it with more damp soil. Firm in the plant well to establish contact between soil ball and new soil.

Be sure to set the plant at the right depth in the pot. If too deep it will not have enough room for root growth; if too high there will not be room in the container to hold water. Fill the pot to within ½ to 1 inch of the top, depending on the amount of water the plant usually requires.

Water thoroughly after planting. A good method to use with small pots is to set them in a pan of water until the soil seems uniformly damp. Water big containers at the surface until water drips from drain holes.

Protect newly potted plants from sun and wind for several days.

## BASIC MIX

### 1 Yard

| | |
|---|---|
| ⅔ yard | ground bark or other organic matter, nitrogen-treated |
| ⅓ yard | silty loam |
| 4 pounds | dry complete fertilizer with 12% nitrogen, half of it in readily available form (identified on the label as *urea* after the nitrogen percentage) |
| 10 pounds | limestone |

### 3 Cubic Feet

| | |
|---|---|
| 2 cu. ft. | ground bark or other organic matter, nitrogen-treated |
| 1 cu. ft. | silty loam |
| ¾ pound | dry complete fertilizer (see above) |
| 2 pounds | limestone |

## SANDY MIX

### 3 Cubic Feet

| | |
|---|---|
| 1½ cu. ft. | organic matter |
| 1½ cu. ft. | sandy soil or sand |
| ¾ pound | dry complete fertilizer (see above) |
| 2 pounds | limestone |

(Organic matter may vary according to regional availability—ground bark, peat moss, rice hulls, and others.)

Mix ingredients thoroughly and store in covered containers for future use.

## ACID MIX

| | |
|---|---|
| 4 or 5 parts | coarse-textured peat moss |
| 1 part | composted oak leaf mold |

## Soil mixes and their requirements

The type of mix you use in your containers is dependent partly on the character of the plant and the kind of character *you* are. If you are a casual gardener with only a few plants in containers, or if you don't want to bother with mixing your own potting soil, the easiest thing is to buy a sack of prepared mix at a nursery. A suitable potting mix must be porous enough to drain well and must contain sufficient nutrients for plant growth. (For details, see page 25.)

**DRAINAGE** • Poor drainage is a common cause of failure in container gardening. Most plants cannot grow in airless, waterlogged soil. It is essential that the mix be sufficiently porous for water to drain readily, yet contain enough organic matter to keep the root zone moist between waterings.

**SALTS** • Harmful salts from water of poor quality, from excessive fertilizer, and salt-laden organic matter will accumulate in poorly drained soil. Too many salts in the soil can stunt plants and finally kill them. Some container plants in particular — azaleas, camellias, rhododendrons, and gardenias — may become chlorotic, show leaf burn, become defoliated, wilted, or collapse entirely.

Excess salts can be detected often by a white deposit on the soil surface. Avoid shallow, frequent watering. Thorough watering at longer intervals is more beneficial to the plant and carries salts on through. To leach out salts periodically, fill the container with water several times until it runs freely out the drainage hole.

**ACID ADDITIVES** • Constant watering leaches out soil and can result in a lessening of soil acidity. Foliage — both old and new — of azaleas, camellias, and other acid-loving plants will begin to take on an overall yellowish cast. To restore acidity, preparations known as acid additives may be combined with water and used as a drench. Acid additives are *not* fertilizers and should be used in addition to a regular feeding program. Carefully follow label directions.

**KINDS OF SOIL MIXES** • Dozens of different soil mixes, several quite complicated, have been offered to gardeners through the years. However, most kinds of plants perform successfully in a basic mix such as that used by the Arboretum Foundation-*Sunset Magazine* Demonstration Home Gardens at the Los Angeles State and County Arboretum. This mix is described on the chart on this page. For plants requiring an acid or sandy soil, the mix is varied somewhat. Ingredients and amounts for the basic mix and its variations are given as a checklist for making up 1 yard or a smaller 3 cubic foot batch.

## REPOTTING

When a plant has filled the pot with its roots, it usually should be shifted to a larger container. Exceptions, of course, are bonsai, which are often root-pruned and returned to the same container, and certain plants, like agapanthus and clivia, which bloom best with crowded roots.

After two years most plants are likely to be root-bound and in need of fresh soil. The plant is ready when its roots show through the drain hole or when, after the plant has been knocked out of its pot, you find roots matted on the outside of the root ball.

If you run an old table knife around the root ball to loosen the damp soil it will be easy to tip out of the pot. Turn the pot upside down, supporting the top of the root ball with your hand. Rap the pot lip sharply on a firm surface to loosen the root ball so that it can slide out of the pot. If the plant doesn't need transplanting slide it back into the pot and rap the bottom sharply to firm the ball of soil. Do not press the ball back in; you might damage the roots or compact the soil.

If the ball is badly entwined with roots, scribe it in several places and follow the potting directions on page 22.

Often pot-bound plants need some of the outer roots and soil sliced off to stimulate growth of new roots into fresh soil. See page 22.

## Transplanting from cans

To make sure that the soil ball doesn't break up when the can is pulled away from it, water the plant thoroughly the day before planting.

Slit the sides of the can and spread it open. Place one hand under the root ball and one hand on top, and lift out the plant.

Cover the drains with pottery or screen, cushion the container bottom with potting mix, and gently set the plant in. Properly position the root ball so the top is sufficiently below the rim of the container to provide room for water. Fill in the space between the root ball and tub sides with soil. Settle in with water.

## Planting burlapped plants

Gentle handling is the main requirement in setting a balled and burlapped shrub or tree in a container.

Before planting, soak the burlapped ball in water until bubbles stop rising. Lower the ball into the tub, setting it gently on a soft bed of potting soil. Support the bottom of the ball with your hands. Never use the trunk as a handle.

After you have adjusted the top of the ball to come within about 2 inches below the top of the container, pack soil between the ball and container sides until it is about three-quarters full. Soak with water and fill in the rest of the space. Just before covering over the top of the root ball, cut the twine that secures the burlap around the trunk. The burlap will rot away in time. Soak with a generous watering.

1. SHRUB READY for transplanting. Cut both sides of can with cutters. Carefully lay plant on side for easy removal of can.

2. REMOVE LOOSE SOIL around roots. Cover drain holes with pottery, carefully position shrub on cushion of soil mix.

3. FILL IN SPACE between root ball and sides of tub with soil mix. Leave one and a half inches at top for watering space.

## MOVING SMALL PLANTS INTO LARGER QUARTERS

*PLANTS USUALLY are moved into pots one size larger. Score rootbound ball with knife, making ¼-inch cuts. Place pot piece over drain.*

*FIRM IN SOIL around edges of plant. Thoroughly water both root ball and new soil. Drench with all-purpose insecticide.*

## REMOVING PLANTS FROM LARGE CONTAINERS

*ROOT BALLS of some large plants can be floated out of their containers by forcing water through the drain hole in the bottom.*

*REMOVE STUBBORN plants by letting soil dry slightly so ball slides out easily. Tap cloth-protected rim with mallet, pull gently to remove.*

## ROOT PRUNING, RETURNING TO ORIGINAL CONTAINER

 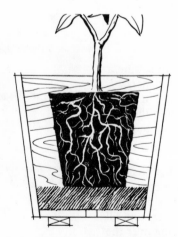 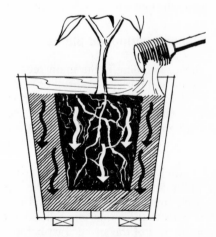

*REMOVE PLANT from container, shave off a few inches of root ball with sharp knife (1 inch on small plants, 4 or 5 inches on large ones). Score root ball. Place on layer of soil mix and fill in to within an inch or two of the container top. Water well.*

## WATERING

All container plants need more water than their counterparts planted in the open ground, where roots can grow down or outward into soil which is moist. But a potted plant is a dependent captive, restricted by the area of the container, and demands greater care. Observe your plants and inspect the soil to determine when and how much water they need.

The faster a plant grows, the more water it needs. You should expect to water most plants daily on hot days, but do not neglect watering during the winter. Pots under eaves and overhangs often suffer from lack of water during rainy seasons because gardeners assume they don't need it at those times. Neither are fog and dew substitutes for water.

Once the soil in a container dries out completely, the soil shrinks and water naturally takes the course between the dry, shrunken root ball and the sides of the pot. It runs out the drain hole without ever penetrating the soil.

*WATER RUNS down sides and out drain when a root ball gets too dry. Add new soil at sides.*

To bring potted plants into full water capacity so that they will take up a water supply *evenly,* halfway submerge pots in a pail of water until the soil stops bubbling, indicating that water has taken the place of air in the structure of the soil.

Don't keep the soil constantly soaked. Water thoroughly but allow enough time between waterings for the plant to take up a good portion of the water in the soil. Test the soil by feeling it or lifting the container. If the potting mix feels wet or if the pot is comparatively heavy, there is water in the soil.

Overwatering endangers plant growth in this way: If the soil is waterlogged over a long time, the air will be forced from the soil and the plant will suffocate or drown.

## Vacation watering

Plants drying out during a vacation is a special worry to container gardeners. Possibly the best way to solve the problem is to hire a responsible neighbor around the age of 12 and explain carefully just what you want watered, how much, and when.

Here are suggestions to keep your collection in good shape while you are away. Move the plants to a shady spot and plunge the pots to the rims in a trench or box filled with moist peat moss, ground bark, leaf mold, sawdust, or shavings. Keep a hose with sprinkler attached nearby; some gardeners set the sprinkler so water will cover the entire collection of containers.

*SINK POTS in a trench of damp peat moss or set sprinkler to water entire collection.*

## How to water

Surface watering with a gentle stream from a hose or watering tube probably is the easiest method.

Caution: Hot water from a hose which has been lying in the summer sun can wilt or sometimes destroy the plants it reaches.

Pots also can be watered from below by placing them in another container partially filled with water. You will find that wooden boxes generally need less moisture than unglazed clay pots and that containers placed in groups stay damp longer than those standing alone. Pot-bound plants dry out fastest. Some plants, such as fuchsias, benefit from foliage spraying (which also helps keep down the spider mite infestation). See the next page for easy watering ideas.

*FOLIAGE watering deflects water away from container.*

*STRONG blast washes out soil. Use soft flow of water.*

*SET pots on gravel bed to avoid paving stains.*

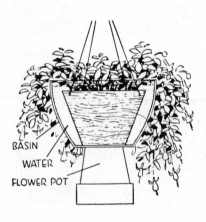

*INVERTED pot prevents harm to hanging branches.*

*TINS hung on chains catch overflow, drips.*

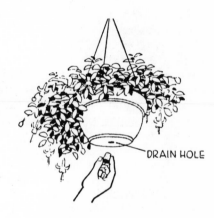

*CORK in drain makes thorough watering possible.*

*HEAVY container has metal drip pan, casters.*

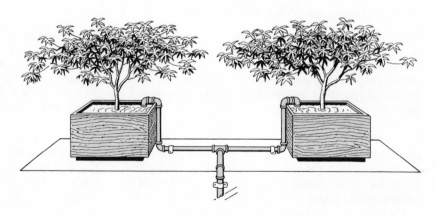

*CONTAINERS often are out of reach for watering. Permanent pipe to each tub and convenient faucet are handy.*

## FEEDING CONTAINER PLANTS

Proper feeding is of prime importance in growing plants in pots. Nutrients constantly are being taken up by the plant and leached out by watering. The faster a plant grows, the more nutrients and water it requires. Consequently, as water is increased so is leaching and loss of nutrients.

Weather is another important factor. At the same time plants are growing fast during warm weather, water is evaporating more rapidly and must be replenished. If during these periods you water too sparingly, harmful salts present in water and soil in some areas concentrate in the root area and damage the plants. Heavy applications of fertilizer, if not followed by thorough watering, are also harmful, especially if the potting mix contains heavy soil.

**FORMULAS FOR FERTILIZING** • The following feeding solution is suggested for *outdoor* plants in pots and boxes during the warm growing season: To 1 gallon of water add 6 teaspoons complete fertilizer (10 percent nitrogen, half in readily available form and the other half slowly available — the label reads *urea* after the nitrogen percentage).

*Indoor* plants, grown in subdued light, do not need as much fertilizer as those outside. Do not overfertilize. Use a weaker solution made with 3 teaspoons to 1 gallon, or a commercial house plant preparation, strictly following label directions.

In warm, sunny weather plants need a stepped-up feeding program. Every 2 weeks feed outdoor pot plants with the above 6-to-1 solution and indoor plants with the weaker, 3 teaspoons to 1 gallon formula.

In colder weather, feed every 6 to 8 weeks depending on the plant's condition. Use a solution of 3 teaspoons complete fertilizer (see above) to 1 gallon of water for both indoor and outdoor plants.

If a plant has specific fertilizer requirements, they will be found under the plant's description in chapter 3, pages 40 to 67.

## PEST AND DISEASE CONTROLS

Since container plants usually are close at hand, it is easy to keep an eye on them and control attacks by pests or diseases before the condition becomes serious. Keep a sprayer or duster handy and apply a multipurpose preparation as soon as you notice signs of infestation. Read label directions carefully; be especially wary when preparing to treat ferns, certain palms, and other plants that are sensitive to spray damage. Use mild solutions, particularly when spraying house plants. Occasional syringing with water or wiping the leaves not only keeps them clean and attractive but helps to discourage build-up of pests such as aphids.

VEGETABLE BRUSH IS HANDY FOR SCRUBBING OUT OLD POTS

SLUGS WILL CURL UP, HIDE IN DRAIN HOLES—YOU'LL HAVE TO DIG THEM OUT WITH A POINTED STICK

*PRECAUTIONS above help control pests. Dirty pots often harbor diseases.*

*CALIBRATED BUCKET is handy for measuring spray, fertilizer. Mark gallon levels with nail polish or waterproof paint.*

*SUREFIRE WAY to keep slugs, other pests from hiding in pot bottom is to cover drain with a square of screening.*

## PRUNING AND TRAINING

The main reason for pruning potted plants is to modify their growth to fit the size of the container. Raised within the confines of a tub or pot, a plant seldom takes on the same character it would if it were set out in the garden and allowed to grow naturally. Therefore, at some time, every potted plant will need pruning, if only to keep down its size.

You also prune for other important reasons — to increase the yield and quality of flowers and fruit; for a special effect; to give the plant a new shape and character, as in training a standard; or to make a miniature out of a bigger plant.

### What to cut off

Before you start pruning a plant for any reason, you must know about terminal buds — the growing buds on the ends of all branches. These tip buds add length to the branches by drawing plant energy during the active growing season. Therefore, if a terminal bud is cut or pinched back, growth stops there and is

diverted instead to other lateral buds. This is an excellent way of getting your plants to behave as you want. For example, a young chrysanthemum will form several stems if you pinch out the top of the single stem when the plant is young. Or, pinch out the terminal buds on every branch of a fuchsia. This will force growth into other buds and you will have bushy growth from three or four new side branches where there was only a single one before.

*WHEN SHORTENING leafy branches, cut just above a leaf. On leafless wood, make cut above cluster of dormant buds.*

Make your cuts above a bud on a small side branch or a main branch, or even to the ground level in the case of multiple stemmed plants. Generally, it is better when you prune to direct the growth of the new branch toward an open space rather than toward another branch. Crossing branches give the plant a cluttered, twiggy look.

In pruning never leave a stub of any length. Use pruners that will make a good clean cut and not leave excess wood to wither and become a home for decay and pests.

Any particular pruning requirements will be found under individual plant's description, pages 40 to 67.

### Pruning for special effects

For profuse blooms on your container plants, prune them in plenty of time for the new flower buds to set. Thin fruit to encourage larger individual size.

Character pruning isn't difficult, but it takes more than a cursory glance to estimate a plant's possibilities. Study it from all angles and probe under the foliage to discover hidden branch structure before you start cutting. On the following pages are pictorial examples of how plants were changed completely in appearance by thoughtful pruning.

*PINCHING OUT the terminal bud (growing tip) diverts growth into lateral branches and keeps the plant full and compact.*

*CONTAINER FUCHSIA. Choose compact kinds. Prune after danger of frost is past.*

*Cut well into old wood to insure new growth on which buds form for summer bloom.*

*After pruning, transplant fuchsia, renew soil and transfer to larger box when necessary.*

*HANGING FUCHSIA. Hangers often are planted three to a box. This is large-leafed 'Anna.'*

*Cut crossing branches back to main stem. Cut last summer's growth to bud inside box rim.*

*After pruning, remove plants from box. Cut back spiraling roots about a third; repot.*

*CAN TO CONTAINER. Pot for rose from 1-gallon can should hold a cubic foot of soil; less for a smaller rose.*

*Lower rose into pot so bud union is level with the rim. Fill in with new potting mix, leaving an inch at top for water.*

*BARE ROOT ROSE. Prune roots so that they reach half the distance to the bottom of pot when bud union is at the rim.*

*Cover drain hole with crockery bit; build cone of soil high enough so bud union of rose is level with rim of pot.*

*LODGEPOLE PINE was started on the way to becoming a bonsai in these four stages. First, lower branches were removed to expose the trunk.*

*STARTING at the base, the trunk is encircled with two strands of wire, which are then separated to single strands at first branch.*

*TRUNK and larger branches gently formed into desired curves. First bend rises gradually from base rather than slanting sharply.*

*WITH WIRING and bending completed, tree has established its individuality. Next step is to transfer it to bonsai container.*

## TRAINING A STANDARD

*'DEBUTANTE' camellia to be trained as standard because of a straight stem, full growth. First, side shoots are removed up to 3½ feet above base.*

*INSERT STAKE. Tie stem in several places below head. Pinch back after flowering for new growth, compactness, more bloom next year.*

## MINIATURE TREE FROM A SHAGGY CONIFER

*THIS LITTLE chamaecyparis obviously has never been close to the pruning shears. Its growth is uneven and shaggy—a plant shaper's dream.*

*A MINIATURE TREE now, it will remain so for some time. Prune away straggly growth to reveal interesting form of branches.*

*COLORADO BLUE SPRUCE, 2½ feet high, just as it came from nursery. Plant should be watered well the day before pruning and potting.*

*CUT DOWN SIDES of can to soil line to reveal bottom branches and to make it easier to prune and shape lower structure of plant.*

*THIN TWIGGY branches to open up top of tree. Remove plant from can, scratch soil from roots with pointed stick; trim to fit container.*

*SET TREE in Japanese pot. Add soil, firm in around roots. Soak pot from below in tub of water, spray top of tree with water.*

## Training climbers and trailers

Almost all vines can be grown for a while in containers, if supported. They are especially useful in paved areas where a plant of some height is needed.

Wisteria, large flowered clematis, and ivy do particularly well. Provide sturdy trellises attached to boxes or use wire "tree" forms for guiding the vines. Annual vines can be trained on wires, heavy string, or poles fastened to boxes in the way shown below.

The only chore, other than the usual watering and feeding, is diligently to pinch back and train the vine during its active growth. Also, keep an eye on root development as some vines will rapidly drive roots right down through the drain holes into the soil if the tub is set on the ground.

See the vine list on page 54 and others suited for growing as trailers in hanging baskets and window boxes on page 56.

*ALUMINUM LOUVERED screen on west side of desert house not only protects plants from sun but from drying winds as well.*

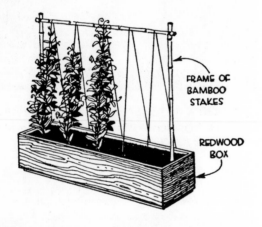

FRAME OF BAMBOO STAKES

REDWOOD BOX

*BAMBOO POLES or dowels make sturdy framework for vines. Tie poles together with plastic twists, thongs. Staple string ends to box.*

## WEATHER PROTECTION

A container exposes a large surface for air to circulate around. Therefore potted plants are more sensitive to changes in temperature than those in the ground. But the portability of some containers cancels out this disadvantage — they can be moved to escape the weather extremes.

Here are ways to protect plants during hot dry weather or hot windy days: Keep plants well watered. Move them if possible to a sheltered spot under an overhang or shade tree. Do not place plants where they will receive reflected heat from paving or walls. In extremely hot areas, plants will not survive unless they are sheltered from heat. See photo.

In cold weather, check newspapers and radio or television reports for frost warnings. Move portable containers to protected spots where they are not exposed to the open sky.

Non-movable plants should be covered with plastic film, burlap, or even newspaper. Try to keep the covering from touching the foliage as heat will be lost from the leaves through the point of contact. Remove the cover in the morning as soon as the temperature rises above freezing.

If a cold spell catches your plants without winter covering and they freeze, take in the portable ones early in the morning before the sun has a chance to thaw them. Place them in the garage or lighted cellar where the air is cold, but above freezing. Allow them to thaw as slowly as possible. Frozen annuals seldom can be revived. Throw them out.

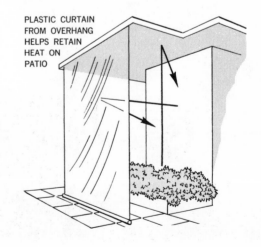

PLASTIC CURTAIN FROM OVERHANG HELPS RETAIN HEAT ON PATIO

*COVERINGS TO CONSERVE stored heat are a good way to keep large containers like permanent planters, window boxes from freezing.*

## MOVING BIG ONES

The first time you bend down to move a good sized container plant, you make two quick discoveries: The container is usually hard to get hold of, and it is much heavier than you expected.

You may start looking for some mechanical aids when you learn that a 12-inch clay pot of freshly watered petunias, for instance, can weigh 65 pounds. A rhododendron in an 18-inch square box weighs up to 200 pounds. The first rule is to move containers *before* watering to eliminate the extra weight.

### Lifting

If you do decide that you are able to lift the container, be certain that you do it with your back straight. Lift the wrong way and you may not lift a container again for a long time! To avoid back strain, keep your back vertical and let your legs do the lifting. Attaching handles to the box also simplifies the job.

### Skids and runners

Dragging a tub over a patio or down a walk is often the hardest way to move it. It isn't so much the weight as the friction that makes it difficult. Often all you need is to reduce the friction and get a good hold on the container.

**WIDE BLADE SHOVEL** • A shovel blade under a heavy tub will slide along well across the ground, lawn, or exposed aggregate. Don't use it on a brick or other surface that might be scratched by the shovel. A wide blade, D-handle coal shovel works well.

*BURLAP BAG used as a skid cloth to move heavy box. Bag will wear through quickly on a rough surface so keep a supply on hand.*

**SKID CLOTH** • Professional movers skid heavy furniture across a surface on tough burlap strips. You can apply the same technique to heavy plant moving by placing a burlap bag or an old throw rug under it. Surprisingly, it will pull quite easily.

**SLED RUNNERS** • A child's sled provides a very satisfactory moving method. You might even want to attach runners permanently to a heavy container.

### Rollers

The use of three or four rollers is the traditional Japanese method of moving a heavy container. Dowels or lengths of 2-inch pipe can be used. As the box is moved along over the dowels, take up a roller from behind and put it in front. Rollers are not easy to use on a slope or rough ground, but you can turn corners easily by fanning out rollers at the turn.

### Wheels

It is hard to operate even a small garden without some wheeled carrier — even a coaster wagon can carry a few clay pots or a small tub. A two-wheeled garden cart is excellent because you can tip it forward and scoop up a sizable boxed plant. A wheelbarrow is built to handle heavier loads. The trick is getting the container in and out without strain. The sketch below shows how.

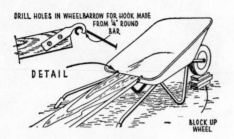

*RAMP FOR MOVING containers is made by hooking board to low end of propped-up wheelbarrow. Pull box in and out on skid cloth.*

Three or four 2-inch industrial casters mounted on 1-inch plywood make satisfactory dollies for heavy loads. It may take two or more men to lift a box a few inches off the ground in order to slip the dolly under it, but the load is easy to move and is well balanced. The casters can be attached permanently to the bottoms of the boxes, but it is a costly process and even the best casters will rust through after a few seasons of exposure.

### Plant rack

Two men can carry a 200-pound pot in the plant rack shown below. The basic frame is three sections of 2-by-4 lumber, two of which form handles. Nail on an 18-inch square of ½-inch thick plywood, with an 8-inch half circle cut out to support the pot. Fit the

cutout section around the pot and lift. Adapt the design to rectangular containers by varying the cutout.

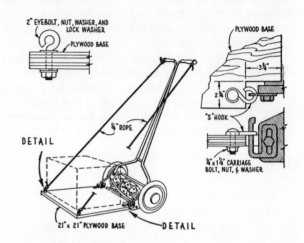

*PLYWOOD BASE for moving boxes is fitted to lawn mower with S hooks. Base is kept level with ropes from handle to hooks in plywood.*

### Hand Truck

A mover's two-wheeled hand truck with long blades will shift very heavy containers to new positions. You can usually rent one from an equipment rental firm. If you have a lawn mower with a handle that can be lowered down past center without lifting the rollers off the ground, you easily can adapt it to use as a hand truck as shown in the sketch above.

In a garden where the effect is dependent on the frequent moving of plants that will bring the best of each season to the foreground, it would be wise to build a special hand truck for containers up to 500 pounds. See photo and sketch below.

*ANYONE with large containers to move would find this rack useful. Vary cutout to adapt rack to carry rectangular containers.*

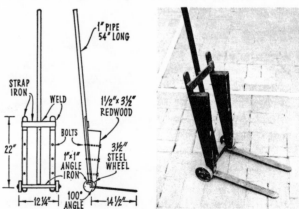

*HUGE TUBBED PLANT can be moved over a fairly level surface with this homemade hand truck. Long lifting blades accommodate box.*

# PROPAGATION

Most gardeners are content to choose a plant they like at a nursery, buy it, and repot it to their liking. However, there are some who enjoy raising container specimens from seedlings, cuttings, layering, or divisions. Below is a checklist of propagation methods and some of the plants that can be grown by each procedure. For details, see Sunset's *Basic Gardening Illustrated*.

**SEED AND SEEDLINGS** • Annuals, perennials, small trees and shrubs for bonsai, tuberous begonias. Prepare a flat of sand and peat moss, or basic potting mix, and follow seed packet instructions for care.

**CUTTINGS** • Philodendron, ivy, azalea, rose, daphne, hydrangea, chrysanthemum, geranium, olive, flowering quince, rhododendron, and succulents. The best cuttings are made in spring or fall from healthy non-flowering side shoots. Trim off lower leaves; dip cut end in hormone powder. For a few cuttings use a pot; for a large number use a flat. Or, put a single cutting in a pot and invert a glass jar over it for a miniature hothouse (occasionally raise the jar to admit air).

**LEAF CUTTINGS** • African violet, peperomia, sansevieria, Rex begonia, gloxinia, many succulents. A leaf will root easily in clean, sharp river sand. Keep moist until rooted and ready to be potted.

**LAYERING** • Juniper, rhododendron, azalea, cotoneaster, daphne, rosemary, maple, flowering quince, zelkova. Select a vigorous low branch and pull it down to the soil level. Either anchor it with wire or cover with soil and hold down with a rock until roots have formed. Cut stem from parent plant.

**DIVISIONS** • Bamboo, chrysanthemum, most bulbous or tuberous plants. Divide a large clump in spring or fall into separate parts. Each root segment is actually a plant in itself. Choose new, healthy ones and pot.

*PUT A JAR over a cutting in a pot to keep atmosphere moist. Keep rooting medium damp. Raise jar occasionally to admit fresh air.*

## DIVIDING A BAMBOO

*1. GRASP A FEW stems and pull steadily as you tap around tub rim with mallet. Root ball should slide out of tub.*

*2. CUT THROUGH tangled mass of thick underground stolons and root ball with ax, sharp spade, or saw. Clumps may be divided again.*

*3. REPLANT each clump in a tub with fresh soil. New shoots should appear in two weeks. Divide golden bamboo every third year.*

## HOUSE PLANTS AND INDOOR-OUTDOOR PLANTS

Although related to container gardening, house plant culture is a type of gardening all its own, requiring some additional information about indoor plants and somewhat more hovering attention on the part of the gardener.

Indoor-outdoor plants fall into still another classification. If you enjoy a certain favorite plant in a handsome pot in your garden, why not bring it inside for a few days or a week and enjoy it close up? One landscape architect told us, "I bring in anything and everything — on a temporary basis, of course."

When you bring a house plant into your home you are transferring it from a greenhouse setting especially suited to a plant's health to an environment not meant for plants but for people. Therefore, you have a special responsibility to reduce the dangers of the new surroundings by providing proper light, water, fertilizer, and drainage.

On these two pages is a short discussion of care of permanent house plants and temporary indoor-outdoor plants. See page 66 for a list of favorite house plants.

**POTTING MIX** • A fine mix is not advisable for house plants as it may pack down hard after the first watering. A good mix that is light and porous consists of: one part loam, one part sand, two parts ground bark or leaf mold.

Also, suitable potting mixes for indoor plants are sold at garden and variety stores in sacks from 1 pound to 25 pounds. Most gardeners use these prepared mixes. It is easy and not too expensive. If you have mix left over, put it in a plastic sack or tight container. It can be stored indefinitely.

**WATERING** • Your control of the moisture supply is the prime requirement for healthy house plants. Both extremes — sogginess about the roots or drying out — can be fatal. The individual plant's need for water is regulated by several factors, including the amount of natural light, room temperature, size of plant, and soil structure. Keep it moist, but not saturated. Test by digging your finger a little under the surface. If soil is no longer moist, it is time to water. Generally, water small pots twice weekly; large containers once a week.

Avoid softened water as the sodium content may be high enough to cause leaf scorching. If the water in your area is softened, give the plant a thorough leaching by setting it in the sink and letting a trickle of water run through it until the soil is soaked.

**DRAINAGE AND WATERING** • House plants to be placed in containers with drain holes are potted the same as any other plants, with just a piece of broken pot over the hole. Do not use a layer of gravel before putting in the potting mix.

*LITTLE HOUSE PLANTS from a supermarket rack, planted in larger 4-inch pots with new soil, quickly show signs of growth.*

However, if the planter does not have drain holes, some allowance must be made for lack of drainage. Place two or more layers of small pebbles over the container bottom and sprinkle charcoal over the pebbles to keep the soil from souring. The charcoal is the same as that used for barbecue fuel, but must be chipped fine. You can chip your own or buy small quantities. Use enough charcoal to cover the pebbles ½ inch deep. Add potting mix.

After planting, indiscriminate day-to-day watering will cause sogginess. Test the soil three or four times a week and water only when the soil underneath is no longer damp.

**LIGHT AND HEAT** • Some plants will survive in dark corners, but all respond to good lighting. If a plant begins to lean toward the light, rotate the pot a quarter-turn weekly.

Try to keep the house temperature consistent; allow fresh air, but avoid cold drafts or warm air from registers or radiators. Caution: sudden changes of temperature can be damaging. Do not set house plants out in the cold rains and be careful about shifting them onto a shaded lanai in the summer unless there is very little difference in temperature between indoors and out.

Humidity in the room is essential. Keep a container of water near the plant to maintain proper humidity at times when air is dry.

**FEEDING** • To keep plants healthy and growing, apply fertilizer according to directions on the label.

Formulas for house plants are widely available. A point to keep in mind: Never feed a sickly plant. Instead check for pests, faulty drainage, overfeeding, or salt burn.

**DUST AND PESTS** • Leaves covered with a film of house dust cannot transpire normally. Once or twice a month clean off the leaves, top and bottom, with a damp sponge or commercial leaf polish. Routine washing also helps keep down insect infestation. You also can buy aerosol cans with insecticides specially formulated for house plants.

## Indoor-outdoor plants

Rotating plants between outdoors and indoors adds a refreshing dimension to both container gardening and interior decoration. Some plants may stay inside only for a special evening or a weekend. But, if the plant is amenable, you may keep it indoors for a week or two, or longer.

**LIGHT** • Light is extremely important. Most outdoor plants will get along best indoors if kept in a cool location near a window. It will also help to give additional light from a lamp, especially during limited winter daylight.

**WATERING** • The needs vary from plant to plant, so check the soil and give a thorough watering when it feels dry. A top dressing of peat moss or ground bark will help keep in moisture.

*EXOTIC BIRD-OF-PARADISE performs well indoors in winter, early spring when blue, orange, and white "birds" bloom.*

*GRACEFUL Mahonia lomariifolia is effective on either side of the entry. Shown indoors here, usually kept outside.*

*WINDSWEPT AND SLANTING was the way this lodgepole pine grew in nature. Pine is twelve inches high. Lacquered base gives balance to bonsai.*

## BONSAI: CARE OF OLD ONES, MAKING NEW ONES

Caring for bonsai (which is pronounced bone-SIGH and means "tray tree") is a great part of the pleasure of owning them. Simple in essence, the careful dwarfing of trees, shrubs, and vines can easily develop from an interesting garden hobby into a consuming garden art.

Bonsai here is described briefly as a facet of indoor-outdoor container gardening, with emphasis on training new plants in the bonsai manner. (See page 59 for a list of recommended bonsai subjects.) Refer to the Sunset book, *Bonsai, Culture and Care of Miniature Trees* for specific information.

**PRUNING** • A miniature tree usually needs only one heavy branch pruning in its life — when the basic form is initially established. From then on, nipping and pinching back will control size and develop the tree's form.

**WATERING** • When bonsai soil begins to dry, water it. Direct a light spray to clean the foliage and to thoroughly soak the soil. Placing plants under a shelter or in semishade and out of the wind helps keep them from drying out. Good drainage is essential.

**FEEDING** • It is a mistake to think that dwarfing a bonsai is achieved by starving it. Dwarfing is controlled by nipping top growth and pruning roots. Follow a regular feeding program. As new spring growth begins, fertilize every other week until leaves are fully open. Then feed once a month. A mild liquid fertilizer, such as house plant food, is fine for bonsai. Carefully follow mixing directions; it is better to overdilute than to use too rich a mixture.

**CONTAINERS** • When roots begin working their way out through the drain holes, it is probably time to repot. You may use the original container again or transplant to another pot. Any simple container that fits the character of the plant is suitable. However, the classic Japanese bonsai pots seem most appropriate. They are available in round, square, oval, and hexagonal shapes in a variety of depths and come in dark brown terra cotta or a number of glazed finishes.

**SOIL** • Potting soil need not be an exotic, mysterious concoction. The following two potting mixes are simple and work well. *Conifers:* ½ sand (not beach sand as it is too salty), ¼ leaf mold, ¼ soil. This mixture gives fast drainage and the good aeration that conifers need. *Broad-leafed plants:* ¼ sand, ¼ leaf mold, ½ soil. This is a slower-draining mix. Using these two formulas enables you to water all your bonsai at the same time and the structure of the soil will take care of the drainage.

Or use a single mixture of 1 part sand, 1 part leaf mold, and 1 part soil; water the conifers less than the other plants.

**PLANTING** • Do not water a bonsai the day before you plan to repot it. Grasp the trunk firmly and rock it gently until the root ball comes free of the pot. Set the root ball in a bucket of vitamin B[1] enriched water to loosen the old soil and to keep the roots moistened and nourished. Poke the old soil away from roots carefully with a pointed stick. Inspect roots carefully and cut away about one-third the mass.

Place bits of broken pottery over the drain holes. Put in a pad of soil mix, then settle in the bonsai, keeping the base of the trunk at desired level. Fill the container with mix, settling it firmly around the roots. Water thoroughly but do not fertilize for at least four or five weeks.

Finish with moss and rocks, which should not be sprinkled over the surface but partially sunk into the soil.

**WIRING AND TRAINING** • The wiring and bending of branches is best done in the spring, when the wood is supple. Use plastic-covered or fabric-coated No. 10-20 house wire. Wind a length of wire around the branch you wish to form, leaving space between each turn but keeping the turns snug against the wood. Carefully bend the wired branch in a wide radius, to avoid the possibility of breaking it.

**MAKING A NEW BONSAI** • On the facing page is an illustrated lesson in creating a new bonsai from a plant in a nursery can.

1. *IN CREATING new bonsai, shop the nurseries for plants of irregular horizontal growth. Camellia in gallon can has possibilities.*

2. *REMOVE PLANT from can and wash dirt from roots in bucket of water. Keep moist at all times as you work.*

3. *IF THE CHOSEN container is small, prune the roots to make them fit. Note amount of material pruned from plant above.*

4. *SOAK POROUS bonsai pot until it stops bubbling. Place a piece of broken pot or small stone over drainage hole.*

5. *POSITION PLANT, firm in potting mix, water thoroughly but gently. Trim excess branches, leave major pruning until plant is established.*

6. *START WIRING at lowest point on tree that you wish to train. The branches are pliable on an actively growing, established tree.*

# PLANTS THAT LIKE TO LIVE IN CONTAINERS

Shrubs and trees • Annuals and perennials • Bulbs • Tubbed vines • Hanging baskets • Succulents and cacti • Specialties—bamboo, bonsai, ferns, herbs, vegetables, pool plants • House plants

Almost any plant you take a fancy to will take well to container living. With this in mind, take a little extra time on your next nursery visit to look for plants with *special* appeal — a nice branching habit, interesting leaves, lovely foliage color. Even if a plant is tender or temperamental, chances are it will thrive in a container because you can place it in a favored location and then proceed to give it the particular treatment it requires.

The plants described on the following pages are especially suited to container culture. Some are familiar favorites, others may be new to you. The categories include: shrubs and trees, annuals and perennials, bulbs, vines, succulents and cacti, plants for hanging baskets, house plants, and specialties such as bamboo, bonsai, ferns, herbs, vegetables, and pool plants.

Remember that these lists are not intended to be all-encompassing. If some other plant intrigues you as a tub subject, give it a try. Because — and here is the real key to the popularity of container gardening —

the opportunities for experimentation, creative endeavor, and personal satisfaction are almost endless.

## SHRUBS AND TREES

Shrubs and trees are basic plants in containers just as they are out in the garden. Evergreen species give an all-year effect and furnish backgrounds for displays of seasonal color, while flowering trees and those with blazing autumn leaves often are in themselves the seasonal color.

An important advantage of growing shrubs and trees in boxes is that you can plant most of them at any time. Nearly all nurseries now have in cans even the deciduous types which once were sold only bare root in winter and spring.

The culture of shrubs varies and will be discussed under individual names. However, in general, most of these should be repotted during their dormant period: evergreens when they are not putting on new growth, deciduous plants when they are out of leaf, and certain flowering shrubs, such as camellias and some azaleas, when they are in full bloom.

It is hazardous to plant trees and shrubs during extremely hot weather unless you carefully shade and water newly planted material. Spraying leaves once or twice a day during a hot spell helps reduce transpiration.

*TREE SEAT in the dappled shade of an old apple tree is setting for wide clay bowls holding colorful annuals. Wood tubs with large shrubs occupy permanent space in landscape.*

## Shrubs and trees with interesting foliage

**ARALIA, JAPANESE** *(Fatsia japonica)* • Big, fanlike leaves and a bold tropical appearance make aralia a popular container plant. Place container in the shade, water and feed regularly. Aralia grows at a moderate rate to 5-8 feet and can be kept smaller in a tub. Plant in a basic soil mix. Repot every 3 years.

**BAY, SWEET** *(Laurus nobilis)* • A classic formal plant for urns, the bay can be pruned into topiary shapes, standards, globes, and cones. It bears the traditional bay leaf of cookery and is also known as Grecian laurel. Plant in a mix that drains well and place container as a background for bright potted annuals. Takes full sun most areas; best in filtered shade in hottest summer climates.

**BEECH** *(Fagus sylvatica)* • An effective container tree, the deciduous beech has smooth gray bark and glossy green leaves which turn brown in the fall. Grows in a basic soil mix. Purple-leafed weeping copper beech can be held for many years in a big pot. Other good kinds are tricolor beech, with green leaves edged in white and pink, and golden beech.

**BOXWOOD** *(Buxus)* • Pleasing, lively green foliage of boxwood is usually trimmed to pyramids, globes, or other formal shapes. Easy to grow in sun or shade in basic mix. In areas of dry heat, plant slow-growing Japanese boxwood. In colder areas use either Korean boxwood or the lustrous English or common boxwood. Shrubs look well in glazed pots, large boxes and tubs, and urns.

**CEDAR, DEODAR** *(Cedrus deodara)* • One of the most widely grown conifers; only the low forms *C. d.* 'Prostrata', which is flat or cascading, and *C. d.* 'Repandens', with stiff horizontal branches, are small enough for lengthy container life. Prune to shape annually in late spring.

**FIR, NORDMANN** *(Abies nordmanniana)* • Twisted and handsome or erect and symmetrical, Nordmann fir will grow in containers for a long time and is better adapted to warmer climates than most firs. Give it generous water and a basic soil mix. Eventually, it will need a large container.

**HEAVENLY BAMBOO, SACRED BAMBOO** *(Nandina domestica)* • Crimson-colored winter leaves, bamboo-like canes, and a lacy, delicate appearance make this a useful, popular container plant. Slow growing to 6-8 feet, it can be held at 3 feet by cutting back oldest canes at ground. With protection from weather extremes, it grows well in most climates in a rich soil mix with ample water. Excellent in a restricted vertical area or wherever an upright, airy effect is needed. Effective in soy tubs, dramatic when night lighted. Can be held for years in a large container.

**JUNIPERS** • Picturesque in branch and trunk, these shrubs come in sizes and shapes to fit nearly any container need. One of the best is slow growing, sage green *Juniperus chinensis* 'San Jose', which spreads 2 feet by 6 feet. Hollywood juniper *J. c.* 'Torulosa', upright to 15 feet, is effective in large containers; *J. c.* 'Weaver' grows to about 3 feet. Plant junipers in basic mix. Spray for aphids, twig borers with malathion and lindane. Control juniper blight with copper spray in July.

**MAPLE, JAPANESE** *(Acer palmatum)* • Airy, delicate Japanese maple has all-year interest — bright red autumn foliage, bare winter branch structure, red leaf growth in spring, and soft green in summer. Thrives under the same conditions as azaleas. Ample watering, periodic feeding, and shelter from heat and dry winds. Slow growing, don't prune when small. A 4-foot tree can remain in a large 18-inch box for 6 to 8 years.

**FLAX, NEW ZEALAND** *(Phormium tenax* 'Atropurpureum')* • Big purple-red swordlike leaves in a fan pattern make this a plant for special display. Grows in nearly every soil or exposure. Leaves are often 9 feet long, but dwarf forms with 6-foot leaves are available.

**NORFOLK ISLAND PINE** *(Araucaria heterophylla)* • This evergreen conifer (not a real pine) grows well in a container for many years and produces a tier of feathery growth annually. In an 8-inch pot it will grow no higher than 4 feet. Use a basic potting soil with good drainage and feed two or three times during growing season with complete fertilizer. Needs a large amount of water in desert areas, winter protection from cold. A good indoor-outdoor choice, it can be kept inside in a moderate temperature — 50 to 60 degrees. Can be propagated from a cutting of a growing tip.

**PALMS, palmlike plants** • Palm's spectacular leaves become doubly dramatic when the plant is placed in an unusual pottery container in a prominent spot. Most young palms prefer the indoors but some tolerate protected outdoor sites in warm climates. Fertilize often. When repotting, use a pot only slightly larger than the one in which the palm was growing.

**Chamaedorea seifrizii** • Distinct cluster palm with feathery leaves for indoors, or outside with shade and protection. Ample moisture is needed.

**Mediterranean fan palm** *(Chamaerops humilis)* • The hardiest palm, but growth is very slow in cold areas.

**Parlor palm** *(Chamaedorea elegans)* • Excellent indoor palm, tolerates crowded conditions, poor light. Repot every two to three years, washing off old soil and starting with fresh mix.

**Sentry palm** *(Howeia belmoreana)* • Arching, feathery leaves are 6-7 feet long. Slow growing, it is an ideal pot plant.

**PHILODENDRON** • Grown for their glossy attractive leaves, philodendrons fall into two groups — hardy for outdoor use in mild climates, and tender for indoor

*FRINGED TIER of ostrich plume branches is produced yearly on Norfolk Island pine.*

*DWARF JUNIPERS and pine in Venetian pots flank Japanese maple displayed in corner of Sunset's patio.*

use. Hardiest of the big-leafed philodendrons for outdoors is *P. selloum,* dramatic in big containers. Often 6-8 feet high.

All philodendrons like rich, well-drained soil. Feed lightly and frequently. See page 67 for indoor philodendrons.

For split-leaf philodendron see *Monstera deliciosa,* on page 67.

**PINE** *(Pinus)* • The presence of a pine or a group of pines adds an immediate woodsy effect to any garden. Generally, they grow best in the sun, planted in a basic, not-too-rich mix that drains well. Most are improved with pruning, some can be dwarfed as bonsai. Feed once or twice a year with complete fertilizer. Never use a fertilizer high in nitrogen.

Here are five especially good pines for containers:

**Bristlecone** *(Pinus aristata)* • Dense, symmetrical; looks mature even when small. Slow growing.

**Japanese black pine** *(P. thunbergiana)* • Irregular and spreading, an excellent pine to prune; favorite bonsai. Hardy.

**Japanese red pine** *(P. densiflora)* • Often forms 2 trunks at soil line. Handsome and informal. Cannot tolerate cold winds.

**Mugho pine** *(P. mugo mughus)* • A favorite for its small size and dense pleasing form. Hardy, but suffers from desert heat.

**Shore pine** *(P. contorta)* • Dense, attractive as 2-foot seedling or mature tree; symmetrical, narrow-crowned. Hardy anywhere.

**PODOCARPUS** • Clean, pest free tree is a good choice for entry or indoor-outdoor plant. It grows slowly for years in a tub, in sun or part shade. Limber branches can be espaliered. Fern pine *(P. gracilior)* has gray-blue leaves; yew pine *(P. macrophyllus)* has broader, bright green leaves.

**SILVERBERRY** *(Elaeagnus pungens)* • Good evergreen plant for portable screening because it is heat and wind resistant, and can be sheared to shape. Reflecting sunlight, rusty dots on the olive green leaves give the plant a special sparkle.

**SPRUCE** *(Picea)* • Can be grown in a tub for years as a living Christmas tree. Provide a cool location and ample water. Spray for aphids monthly from February through May. Try dwarf white spruce *(Picea glauca* 'Conica'), a soft-needled pyramid. Shelter from heat, drying winds. Colorado blue spruce *(P. pungens* 'Glauca') has positive blue color. See page 31.

*SPECTACULAR AZALEAS are favorite subject for containers. Required drainage is good and tubs can be shifted from excess sun.*

*VIBRANT BOUGAINVILLEA 'Temple Fire' thrives on sunny deck in summer, needs winter protection. Bright bloom summer to late fall.*

### Flowering Shrubs and Trees

**AZALEA** • An azalea is one of the most spectacular plants you can put into a pot — superb beauty in flower, handsome foliage out of bloom. Gardeners in nearly every climate (an exception is the desert) where winter temperatures do not fall below minus 15 degrees can grow some kind of azalea in a container. Especially adapted are Belgian Indica and Kurume kinds, but there are about a dozen different groups of azaleas, evergreen and deciduous, in red, pink, salmon, violet, white. The best way to pick one is to visit a nursery during the spring bloom season and find a shape, bloom, and size you want. Your nurseryman will give you details of local hardiness.

Generally, azaleas do best in spongy, acid mix (page 20) in a wind-protected and partly shaded spot. Keep constantly moist but not soggy. Feed with acid plant food (some are labeled "azalea food") every 6 to 8 weeks, three or four times from the *end* of the flowering season until September. Prune at blooming time and pinch back new tips during growing period to keep plants compact.

**BOUGAINVILLEA** • Bushy forms of this evergreen, flowering vine are best suited for containers. In summer use 'Crimson Jewel,' 'La Jolla,' or 'Temple Fire' (all vibrant reds) in a sunny patio, move to protected spot in colder months when temperature threatens at 30 degrees. Plant carefully in basic potting mix without disturbing roots. Fertilize spring and summer. Don't be afraid to prune to shape.

**CAMELLIA** • Exquisite flowers and handsome foliage make camellias container aristocrats. Although colors are limited to reds, pinks, white, and variegations, the kinds and varieties are nearly endless. *C. japonica* is *the* camellia to most gardeners, but *C. sasanqua* with its delicate beauty, spectacular *C. reticulata,* as well as other kinds are worthy container subjects.

If your soil is alkaline, containers are a blessing. Use an acid mix, keeping trunk base just above the soil line. Feed with commercial acid fertilizer in the period after bloom. Follow label directions carefully.

A thick mulch helps to keep camellias constantly moist. Protection from hot sun and winter cold is a must. Camellias combine naturally with azaleas.

The same pot or tub can be home to a camellia for several years. When it is time to remove and root-prune, or move to a bigger tub, the job of repotting always should be done during the dormant season, while the shrub is in bloom. Never repot a camellia in a box with more than a 4-inch clearance between root ball and box wall, as the soil becomes soggy and sour when not reached by roots.

**CRAPE MYRTLE** (*Lagerstroemia indica*) • Crepe paperlike clusters of petals and fall foliage color are features of this deciduous shrub. Flourishes in hot interiors and desert areas but tends to mildew where summers are cool. Locate in full sun in basic mix. Feed moderately, water infrequently but thoroughly. Dwarf forms are best for containers. Prune out twiggy growth while dormant.

*INFORMALLY TRAINED on trellis, camellia shows its white blooms and large leaves to advantage in cool, shady spot.*

*COOL CORNER of brick patio is stage for a star performer—rhododendron 'Alice', with huge clusters of deep pink blooms.*

**DAPHNE** *(Daphne odora)* • Neat and handsome, this evergreen shrub is loved for its winter or spring blossoms with pervasive fragrance. Because daphne is temperamental about watering and absolutely demands a fast draining soil mix, it often is more reliable in a box than in open ground. Slow growing to 2 or 3 feet, it needs morning sun to set blossoms but cannot take hot afternoon sun and heat. Prune during, after bloom.

**FLOWERING FRUIT TREES** • Some deciduous flowering fruit trees, such as peach and almond, are not good container plants because their out-of-bloom appearance is so unimpressive that they almost need to be hidden away. The list below includes not only those with spectacular flowers but redeeming looks when not in blossom.

They require fast draining basic soil mix and regular feeding. Use sprays to control pests or mildew. Prune to shape at bloom time. Remember that these plants are *trees* and should be placed in containers that balance their height. When the tree gets too large for a box, plant it in the open ground.

**Japanese flowering cherry** *(Prunus serrulata)* • Attractive in almost any setting; clouds of incomparable spring blossoms in pink and white.

**Flowering crabapple** *(Malus)* • Choose the small kinds. Least troublesome of the flowering fruit trees, they combine beautifully with spring bulbs, primroses, and summer-blooming, shade-loving plants. Some have attractive small fruits. Three years is the average stay of a 5 or 6-foot crabapple in a 15-inch box.

**Flowering plum** *(Prunus blireiana)* • Leaves are reddish purple and flowers are pink and fragrant. A 3-foot tree can stay in a 12-inch tub for two years.

**Flowering quince** *(Chaenomeles)* • Neatly clothed in white, pink, or red blooms in earliest spring, flowering quince has angular, picturesque branch structure. Excellent container plant, it is hardy, easy to grow. Place in a basic mix; prune at bloom time. C. 'Contorta' is a good low, twisted form.

The dwarf forms of trees with edible fruit are also excellent container subjects. See page 87.

**FUCHSIA** • Popular in lush, cool spots in the garden or under a shady overhang, fuchsias are dependable deciduous shrubs. They require porous, water-retentive, but fast-draining potting mix and heavy watering. Flowers — pink, white, red, or violet — are always suspended and in a variety of sizes. Put the containers where you can watch the hummingbirds visit them.

In frostless areas, prune back in spring to within two buds of previous summer's growth; in cold-winter areas prune lightly after last frost to remove twiggy growth. Cut back into live wood.

Repot at least every other year. Select upright kinds for boxes and tubs, trailing kinds for hanging baskets.

Easily propagated by cuttings, several 2 to 3-inch-long tips can be rooted in damp sand and later placed in pots or hanging baskets for summer bloom. Every ten days or two weeks apply a light dose of complete fertilizer to keep blooms coming.

Fuchsias grow best in cool summer climates, but you can create a pleasant atmosphere for them in warm areas with wind and sun protection and attentive watering — often twice a day. In cold winter areas, containers should be moved to a protected area and heavily mulched.

**GARDENIA** • The attractive qualities of gardenias — glossy evergreen leaves and deeply fragrant waxy white blooms — are most apparent where summer days and nights are warm. In cool areas, the box can be shifted somewhat to suit the climate needs of the gardenia.

*G. jasminoides* 'Mystery' is the best known and eventually will reach 3 or 4 feet in a box, as will *G. j.* 'Veitchii'. *G. j.* 'Radicans' reaches only 6 to 12 inches and has inch-wide flowers.

**HYDRANGEA, Bigleaf or Garden** *(Hydrangea macrophylla)* • Few shrubs give a bigger flower display during summer months. Color ranges from white through purple and red. It is easy to grow in a rich, porous soil, but requires heavy, regular watering. Fertilize 3 or 4 times during growing season. Protect against full sun in inland areas. Prune to control size at bloom time. Effective massed in partial shade.

To get blue flowers on pink and red varieties, or keep blue-flowered kinds from turning, treat with a solution of aluminum sulfate (1 tablespoon in a gallon of water); make 2 or 3 applications before the plant blooms.

**LILY-OF-THE-VALLEY SHRUB** *(Pieris japonica)* • Elegant year-around appearance makes this an excellent evergreen shrub for entry. Clusters of white, pearl-like flowers appear in spring. New leaves unfold bronzy pink, and clusters of green-pink buds hang from branches in fall and winter. It needs generous watering and protection from sun and wind. A relative of rhododendrons and azaleas, it has the same cultural needs. Dwarf forms are available. It is not adapted to desert climates.

**OLEANDER** • A basic evergreen shrub for hot inlands and desert. Big clusters of pink, white, yellow, or red blooms appear from May until October. One of the best shrubs for warm, sunny patios. With pruning it can be held to moderate size in a tub for years. Needs protection from cold winters. A caution: all parts are poisonous if eaten.

**RHODODENDRON** • There probably is no plant you can put into a container that will bring forth more delighted exclamations than a blooming rhododendron. A well-tended evergreen rhododendron can be a flower extravaganza in blood red, blush pink, creamy white, yellow, and near-blue — and all variations of shades in between. It combines well with — and has the same growing requirements as — lily-of-the-valley shrub, azaleas, and many ferns. Put tubbed rhododendrons under trees that give a filtered shade, near protected entryways, on north and east sides of buildings and fences, and under lath overhangs.

Use a rich acid soil (see page 20) that can be kept constantly moist yet will also drain well. *If drainage is good,* it is almost impossible to overwater a rhododendron. Feed monthly after bloom until August with commercial acid fertilizer.

*CLUSTER OF HYDRANGEAS in clay pots blooms impressively during summer months; requires heavy watering. Use small kinds in containers.*

*LILY-OF-THE-VALLEY SHRUB is laden with long drooping clusters of white, pearl-like flowers in spring. New foliage is bronzy-pink.*

For containers, select mainly low-growing kinds. White 'Bric-a-Brac' and 'Blue Diamond' are excellent varieties growing to about 3 feet.

**ROSE** *(Rosa)* • Planting a rose in a container enables you to bring the world's favorite flower right up to where you can enjoy each bloom through every phase of its unfolding.

First, buy only healthy, top quality roses suited to your climate and plant them in a basic soil mix in boxes, tubs, or large pots. In planting roses, remember that their roots should not be cramped. Use containers large enough to accommodate the roots when they are spread out.

Locate in full sun or half-day sun where air moves freely. Feed with a complete fertilizer just as growth begins in spring, next after the main bloom period, and again when the plant begins to put out growth for a fall crop of flowers. Soak thoroughly every few days, even daily during hot spells. For rose pruning and pest and disease control, see the *Sunset* book, *How to Grow Roses.*

Roses have vigorous root systems. Every three or four years, remove from containers during the winter dormant season and use a sharp knife to trim 2 or 3 inches from the root-matted sides and bottom of the root ball. Replace in the same tub, or a larger one if you wish, adding fresh new soil mix at the bottom and sides of the tub. Soak thoroughly, and apply a mulch to retain moisture.

Lower growing roses that produce flowers in large clusters, such as the Floribundas and Polyanthas, are especially popular for containers. 'The Fairy', pink, and 'Margo Koster', coral orange, are two good Polyanthas; each has a cascading habit that is especially effective for containers. 'Sarabande', red; 'Roman Holiday', orange red; and 'Border Gem', yellow, are excellent Floribundas. Hybrid Teas will also do well in containers, but for pleasing effect it is best to avoid the tall, lanky varieties.

Miniature roses are delightful, and are particularly popular as indoor-outdoor plants. 'Eleanor', with tiny pink double flowers, is one of many excellent varieties.

**SHRIMP PLANT** *(Beloperone guttata)* • The unusual appearance of bronzy-orange "shrimps" from overlapping bracts makes this an interesting plant for entry or patio. It will grow to a 3 or 4-foot mound but can be kept lower and more compact by diligent pinching in early growth. Use a basic potting mix and feed with a complete fertilizer. A Mexican native, shrimp plant needs winter protection in colder areas.

**YESTERDAY-TODAY-AND-TOMORROW** *(Brunfelsia calycina floribunda)* • The flowers are purple one day, violet the next, and near-white the next — hence the name. A handsome evergreen, it does best in slightly acid, rich soil mix. Responds to regular watering and feeding with complete fertilizer. Can be held to 3 feet by pruning. Combine with camellias and azaleas.

**YUCCA RECURVIFOLIA** • An excellent dramatic choice for a desert garden with succulents and cacti, this yucca has long, blue-gray leaves and a white summer flower spike. Easy to grow in a sandy mix. See page 20.

*THREE MINIATURE ROSES repotted from 4-inch pots to a 10-inch fern pot will produce a rounded mass of tiny blooms.*

*CHANGING COLORS of yesterday-today-and-tomorrow's flowers make this shrub popular for containers. Combines well with camellias, azaleas.*

## Shrubs and Trees with Fruit or Berries

**CITRUS, dwarf varieties** • With glossy evergreen foliage, fragrant blossoms, and colorful fruit, dwarf citrus are ideal mild-winter container trees. With a little extra care, you can bring them inside and create a climate to suit them.

Daily watering may be necessary in hot weather. A 2-inch pebble mulch is helpful. Use a high-nitrogen (citrus) fertilizer in late winter, June, and again in August. For most dwarf citrus, the containers should be about 18 inches across.

**Kumquat** • 'Nagami', 3 to 4 feet, bears 1-inch orange fruit in autumn.

**Lemon** • 'Eureka' is the standard commercial lemon. 'Meyer', tangy and juicy, bears early.

**Lime** • 'Bearss' is thorny, bears lemon-size fruit.

**Mandarin orange** (tangerine) • 'Dancy' produces traditional Christmas fruit. 'Kinnow' ripens in spring and is a good citrus for any climate.

**Orange** • 'Robertson', good in warm interior climates; heavy bearing in winter. 'Shamouti' is beautiful in form and foliage; bears heavily in spring.

**'Rangpur' lime** • Really a sour acid mandarin orange. Colorful year-around fruit.

*AROMATIC YELLOW FRUITS with flavor of lime are borne year around on dwarf Eustis limequat in mild areas. Like all citrus, sensitive to frost.*

**Tangelo** • Red-pulped fruit similar to grapefruit. Does well in coastal valleys.

**COTONEASTER** • Stiffly angled branches of rock cotoneaster *(C. horizontalis)* make it a good candidate for a tubbed espalier or traffic barrier. *C. congesta* is slow growing, ground hugging, does well in hot and cold climates. Both have small leaves, whitish flowers, red berries. All grow vigorously and thrive with little care.

**FRUIT TREES, dwarf varieties** • The dwarf kinds of trees that bear edible fruit are good in large containers. The spring blossoms are a bonus. See peach tree on page 87.

**GUAVA** • Subtropical pineapple guava *(Feijoa sellowiana)* bears bland, pineapple-flavored fruit in autumn. Prune to shape in spring. For mild-winter climates. Strawberry guava *(Psidium cattleianum)* is best in a rich mix. Useful as a portable screen, it is also a fine bonsai subject. Sweet-tart red fruit in winter.

**HOLLY** *(Ilex)* • A pot of growing holly, with or without traditional berries, is an attractive indoor-outdoor plant — especially at holiday time. Usually both male and female plants must be planted for the female to bear fruit. Holly prefers a rich, slightly acid mix and a spot in the sun. Water amply and use a mulch. Spray twice a year to control pests. Chinese holly *(I. cornuta* 'Burfordii Nana') has exceptionally large berries and self-pollinates; English holly *(I. aquifolium)* is the traditional Christmas holly.

**LOQUAT** *(Eriobotrya japonica)* • Big, crisp, glossy, leathery leaves make this a good evergreen tubbed tree for a patio. Orange fruit is sweet and aromatic. Loquat thrives on moisture. Sun or shade. Fireblight is a danger.

**MAHONIA LOMARIIFOLIA** • Interesting, vertical branch structure and spiny, glossy leaves. Yellow flower clusters appear in winter and are followed by powdery blue berries. Needs afternoon shade.

**OREGON GRAPE** *(Mahonia aquifolium)* • A serviceable, substantial shrub, it takes exposure and can be pruned to stay well under 6 feet. Glossy leaves turn red in autumn; spring flowers followed by blue-black fruit that makes good jelly.

**POMEGRANATE** *(Punica granatum)* • Burnished red globe shaped fruits appear among bright golden leaves in the fall; showy blooms in spring. Pomegranate tolerates great heat and needs sun for fruit production. *P.* 'Wonderful' and *P.* 'Sweet' have excellent fruit. *P.* 'Nana' is a dense, 3-foot dwarf.

**PYRACANTHA** • Grown for bright berries and rugged, informal effect, pyracanthas do well in full sun and a basic soil mix just on the dry side. *P.* 'Rosedale' espaliers well, has bright red berries clustering its branches. *P.* 'Tiny Tim' reaches only 3 feet, nearly thornless. Berries are red.

## ANNUALS AND PERENNIALS

Most annuals and perennials can be grown in containers, but some are better adapted than others. Generally, annuals are attractive only while in bloom and should be considered temporary pot plants. A few perennials, such as geranium, bird of paradise, and agapanthus, have redeeming foliage and make pleasant year-around displays.

### Annuals — temporary, one-season color

Using a basic potting mix, plant in spring from flats when plants are available at your nursery. Some are particularly easy to grow from seed. Sow seeds rather lavishly directly into the soil in the container, which has been soaked until the potting mix is moist to the top. Cover seeds lightly with half sand and half peat moss or ground bark sifted through a fine screen. Keep pots shaded until all seeds have germinated. Thin out seedlings if too crowded; however, for mass and short-season display (as with sweet alyssum) little thinning is necessary.

In general, it is a good idea to make a light monthly application of complete fertilizer. Start two weeks after potting transplants.

All annuals on this list do well in sun and light afternoon shade, and bloom in spring and summer, unless otherwise noted. When planted alone, most of these are excellent in clay pots or other small containers. However, don't forget the effect of several kinds planted in a single large box.

**AGERATUM** • Lavender-blue floss flowers in dwarf forms combine well with petunias; also effective interplanted with alyssum.

**ALYSSUM, SWEET** • Mounds of fragrant alyssum make a quick-growing flounce around a tall plant in a pot. Sow in place or use plants from flats.

**BALSAM** (*Impatiens*) • Plant these old-time favorites two or three to a pot and set them under a tree or against a background that will show off their dazzling color. Spreading dwarfs and 2-foot kinds.

**BROWALLIA** • Lovely blue flowers bloom in partial shade from summer into fall. Group pots in front of fuchsias, hydrangeas.

**CALENDULA** • Cheery orange, yellow, apricot, or tangerine blooms give a mid-winter garden a bright dash of color. Pinch back tall main stem to encourage branching and more flowers.

**CANDYTUFT** (*Iberis*) • Sow seeds in late fall or early spring in pots; group with daffodils, Dutch iris, tulips or other bulbs. The mounding plants have white, pink, lilac, rose, or salmon flowers.

**COCKSCOMB** (*Celosia*) • A box of fiery red cockscomb plumes can be an arresting sight combined with white petunias. Use in full sun.

**COLEUS** • The colorful foliage brightens shaded patios in summer. Start plants from cuttings. Also a popular house plant; reaches 2 to 3 feet.

**LOBELIA** • Cluster pots of mounding or graceful, trailing blue lobelia at a doorway, on decks, terraces, or in patios. Invaluable as a cascade edging in big containers. Part shade inland; sun along coast.

*SPRING TO FALL box of blooms features yellow and purple violas, white alyssum. Geraniums in pots are changeable background for annuals.*

*PLANTING POCKET filled with golden calendulas, which stand up well in heat. Keep plants blooming until fall by picking flowers.*

*TRIO OF POTS with compact marigold 'Spun Gold'
produces large, 3-inch blooms all through summer.
Dwarf kinds also good in pots.*

*LARGE TEACUP-SIZED Oriental pots are unusual
containers for yellow pansies, which combine well
with other annuals, bulbs, fresh spring foliage.*

**MARIGOLD** • Tall robust plants for large containers;
small French marigolds for smaller containers, or
massing in large boxes. All bloom through summer
into fall.

**NASTURTIUM** • One of the easiest to grow in pots.
Sow directly in container, thin to number needed; or
sow in small pots or bands and transplant into permanent containers. Trailing types make good hangers.

**NEMESIA** • Excellent as a bulb cover. Colorful ¾-
inch flowers on 10 to 18-inch-high plants. Mass plant
in large pots or boxes. Effective with violas, pansies,
dwarf white sweet alyssum.

**NICOTIANA** • Place a group of potted upright nicotiana plants on a terrace you use on summer evenings.
*Nicotiana alata* 'Grandiflora,' 2-3 feet high, has large,
very fragrant white flowers; smaller white flowers of
*N. suaveolens* are most fragrant of all.

**PANSY, VIOLA** • Springtime isn't complete without
these favorites. They are lovely alone and also combine nicely with most other spring blooms.

**PETUNIA** • Invaluable for all kinds of containers;
easy to grow. Trailing varieties are best for hanging
baskets and large, tall containers. Give light afternoon
shade in hot areas.

**PINK** *(Dianthus)* • Several pots of pinks add spicy
fragrance and a jaunty look to a terrace or patio.

**PRIMROSE** *(Primula)* • Mass boxes of lacy fairy
primrose *(P. malacoides)* for winter-spring color in
mild areas. Polyanthus primroses *(P. polyantha)* come
in brilliant and pastel colors and bloom from winter
to spring. All primroses need a cool climate, moist
rich soil, and some shade in inland areas.

**SCARLET SAGE** *(Salvia)* • The blazing red color
combines best with gray-foliaged or white-flowered
plants. Taller (to 3 feet) and dwarf (1-foot) varieties
available.

**SWEET PEA** • Plant self-supporting bush types of
this old favorite in containers. Both Knee-Hi and Bijou
flower profusely. For sweet pea containers and supports, see page 32.

**VERBENA** • Fast-growing, sun-and-heat-loving, there
is a verbena color that will contrast as ground cover
with nearly any container plant you may have.

**ZINNIA** • Hot weather, full sun favorites for dazzling
summer color. Try the compact, small flowered
Thumbelina, Tom Thumb, or even some of the taller
kinds if you have a large, deep box.

### Perennials — some look good all year around, others have a flash of seasonal glory

Colorful, easy-to-grow perennials fill a flower color
gap in a mid-summer garden. There is a special advantage to growing them in pots — you can bring
them on-stage when they are at their peak. When
bloom is finished, cut back the plant and put it behind
the scene (possibly sink the pots in open ground in
a secluded part of the garden).

In spring or fall, pot up perennials in rich soil and
place in a sunny location unless noted below. When
new growth appears, start feeding with complete fertilizer; apply monthly until flowers show color.

**AGAPANTHUS** • Excellent permanent container
plants; will bloom even when rootbound. A clump of
agapanthus in a large aggregate container is a dramatic

planting. Dwarf forms, such as 'Peter Pan' or 'My Joy' are a better size for smaller containers; or they can be grouped in large ones. Will take part shade.

**ASPARAGUS FERN** (*Asparagus plumosus*) • Dark green, feathery foliage resembles fern fronds. Plant dwarf kinds in pots, using rich soil; feed in spring with complete fertilizer. Cut back old shoots in spring.

**ASTER** • Compact dwarfs make cushiony mounds of color with taller plants in large containers. Divide clumps every two years.

**BEGONIA, Bedding or Wax** • Bedding begonias are useful for flower and foliage color in summer, fall. Plant in half peat moss, ground bark, or leaf mold, and sandy soil. Set pots in partial shade and protect from wind. See Begonia, Tuberous, page 52.

**BIRD OF PARADISE** (*Strelitzia reginae*) • Spectacular orange, blue, and white blooms startlingly like tropical birds appear throughout the year above strap-shaped leaves. Feed frequently, heavily. Large, crowded clumps do best, so divide infrequently. Plants may reach 5 feet. See page 37.

**CARNATION** (*Dianthus*) • Border carnations bloom profusely, are bushier, lower than florists' kinds and look better in pots. Grow in full sun.

**CHRYSANTHEMUM** • There is no monotony in an autumn garden filled with boxes of chrysanthemums. The shapes, sizes, and colors available seem endless. Most kinds do best in sun and vary from 10 inches to 3 feet. The cushion types grow in 12-inch compact mounds and bloom profusely. Or they can be pruned into standard forms.

**CINERARIA** (*Senecio cruentus*) • Grow large flowered, dwarf kinds in big pots for patio display in late winter or early spring in mild climates, late spring and early summer in colder areas. Plant in moist, rich soil; locate in shade.

**GERANIUM** (*Pelargonium*) • The most bourgeois plant in the garden — everyone knows it and nearly everyone has one. Some are scented, others have fancy leaves and bright bloom, and look good throughout the year. Most are easy to grow in basic soil kept a bit on the dry side. Repot when somewhat rootbound. Pinch tips for bushiness.

**MARGUERITE** (*Chrysanthemum frutescens*) • Small plants in spring will be huge by summer and blanketed with daisy-like blooms. Place in full sun. Replace every 2 or 3 years with new plants from cuttings. Prune frequently but *lightly* for continued bloom.

**PLANTAIN LILY** (*Hosta*) • Trumpet-shaped flowers top thin spikes above lush, heart-shaped leaves. A striking plant for massing around a pool in shady or semi-shady spots. Feeding once a year brings on extra leafy splendor. Becomes completely dormant in winter; new spring growth especially vulnerable to snails and slugs.

*BLUE MARGUERITE, planted in spring, is huge by summer. Produces continuous bloom for months if pruned lightly after each flowering.*

*STATELY FLOWER STALKS of agapanthus show off well in large fluted concrete container. Foliage is attractive all year.*

*LARGE-CUPPED DAFFODILS in Spanish fern pots enhance a terrace in spring. Filtered shade helps prolong bloom and prevent fading.*

## BULBS — FOR A FLOWER SHOW IN CONTAINERS

Potted bulbs offer the advantage of spectacular seasonal color that can be carried on-stage and taken away when the show is ended.

### Culture

For spring bloom, plant unblemished No. 1 bulbs or tubers in late fall. Use a porous mix of equal parts loam, coarse sand, and peat moss, ground bark, or leaf mold. Place a piece of broken crock over the drainage hole. Set bulbs in pots or other containers so the tips are level with or just below the surface of the soil. Soak pots and place them — covered with several inches of moist peat, sand, sawdust, or wood shavings, or boards or inverted flats — in a cool, dark place where the roots will be encouraged to form. After 8 to 12 weeks, check to see if roots are starting to emerge from the drainage hole. If so, remove covering and place pots in a light spot where top growth will develop. When tops are green, put plants in full sun.

Water regularly until after flowering and apply balanced fertilizer two or three times after leaves form. After blooming, foliage should be left on until completely yellowed. Withhold water and tip out bulbs when dry to be stored and planted out in the open garden next season. Bulbs that have been pot forced seldom give as big blooms the second year.

**AMARYLLIS** • Pot bulbs of these unusually beautiful container plants in November in rich sandy loam to which complete fertilizer (1 teaspoon to a 6-inch pot) has been added. Leave top half of bulb above soil. Colors range from red to soft pink and green-tinged white. Amaryllis blooms from December to June, depending on kind.

**BEGONIA, Tuberous** • Varying remarkably in size, shape, and color, begonias bloom July through September. Start tubers in coarse leaf mold in late January or early February when pink buds appear. When growth is 3 inches high transplant to pots or wooden boxes — one to a 6 or 8-inch container in a porous fast-draining mix consisting of ⅔ leaf mold and ⅓ coarse sand. Ready-made mixes containing large amounts of organic matter are suitable. Keep moist in part shade.

**BLOOD LILY** *(Haemanthus katherinae)* • White bulbs with red streaks — hence the name. Large red blooms on 2-foot stems. Put one bulb in 10-inch pot in rich mix in winter. Water lightly and keep indoors in 70° temperature until leaves appear (8-10 weeks). Move outdoors to shelter, water thoroughly, feed monthly. Do not repot next season; merely add new soil mix on top.

**CANNA, Pfitzer's Dwarf** • Exotic-looking, 30-inch tall cannas are best potted in groups of single colors in large tubs. Plant in rich soil in mid-spring for late summer bloom. Bloom colors range from white to orange and red; leaves are tropical looking.

**CROCUS** • Plant hardy corms in boxes in fall and reap a rich reward of color in spring. Showy, colorful little cups appear above grass-like clumps of leaves from September to February, depending on species. Adapted to sun or light shade. Withhold water in summer.

**CYCLAMEN, Florist** *(C. persicum)* • Large flowers appear high above rounded leaves from late fall to late spring. In September, plant in rich porous mix, with the upper half of the tuber above soil level. Good for replacing tuberous begonias when their bloom is finished in late summer.

**DAFFODIL** • Easiest to grow and most popular of all the bulbs, daffodils are consistently good performers. In fall plant early and late kinds for a long season of color — December to April. Excellent in wood boxes or terra cotta pots to give sparkle to a terrace or patio, on steps, along paths, near entry.

**FREESIA** • Sweetly fragrant freesias are carried on wiry stems above grass-like leaves in early spring. Plant several of one color in individual pots from August to November. Repot after bloom when clumps get crowded. Tender in cold climates; grow indoors or in cold frames until frosts are past.

**HYACINTH** • Size of bulb is directly related to size of flower spike, so buy big (exhibition) bulbs for potting. Flowers are waxy, fragrant, and bell-like in white and cream through shades of red, purple, blue. Excellent for cold-winter areas, they also may be grown indoors in water in a special hyacinth glass. Plant in fall

*RICH BLUE DUTCH IRIS planted in thick, squat box. Bulbs placed 2 inches apart and 3 inches deep. Plant in fall for spring bloom.*

for spring bloom. If buds appear while stems are short, put cardboard cone or inverted pot (with drainage hole) over the top of the plant to draw stems up.

**IRIS** • With the exception of extremely tall kinds, iris are showy, graceful additions to a container garden. The bulbous iris, including Dutch, English, and Wedgwood are especially good. In late fall, plant five bulbs to a 6-inch pot. Dwarf and miniature varieties of rhizomatous iris adapt to containers. See Pool Plants, page 64, for Japanese iris.

**KAFIR LILY** *(Clivia miniata)* • Clusters of orange trumpet flowers rise above clumps of lustrous strap-shaped leaves in winter or early spring. Handsome alone or with other shade plants. Plant in rich soil with top of tuber above soil line. Fertilize two or three times during growth. Leave undivided for several years.

**LILY** *(Lilium)* • For late spring and summer color in containers, lilies are unbeatable. Depending on its size, place one bulb in a deep 5 or 7-inch pot; or several bulbs in larger boxes and tubs, with 2 or 3 inches between each bulb. Use sand, loam, peat moss in equal parts. Place where pots are shaded and blooming top has filtered sun. Water plentifully while in bloom and feed weekly. Among superb lilies for containers are 'Enchantment', with orange-red flowers, Henryi hybrids, *L. longiflorus* and hybrids, *L. speciosum* and hybrids. After bloom, never allow to dry out completely. Repot in late fall in fresh mix.

**NERINE** • Iridescent pink or scarlet wispy flowers with crinkly petals bloom on 1 to 2-foot stems from August through January, depending on kind. Plant August-December, one bulb to a 4-inch pot or three

to a 6-inch pot. Nerine flowers best when roots are crowded. Like amaryllis, only the lower half of the bulb should be covered with soil.

**RANUNCULUS** • Spring flowers look like jumbo sized single, semi-double, or fully double buttercups and come in a vivid array of yellow, orange, red, pink, cream, and white. Start the bone-hard, clawlike tubers in flats of moist sand or perlite. When tops are 3 inches high, set three plants in a 5 to 7-inch pot; or plant a dozen or more in tub or large box. Or, plant tubers directly in pots, several to a pot, about an inch below soil level. It is a good idea to soak the tubers in water for several hours prior to planting. Water regularly during the growing season; feed with complete liquid fertilizer once a month.

**SCILLA** • For a fresh springtime display intermingle pots of nodding bluebells with your containers of golden daffodils. Plant in autumn, usually six bulbs to a 5 or 6-inch pot. Foot-tall Peruvian scilla has a large bulb; place one in a 6-inch pot.

**TULIP** • Stately and formal, dainty and whimsical, or bordering on bizarre (depending on the kind), most tulips display well in containers. Plant in October unless weather is still warm. Tulips require open sky and sun and grow best in a rich, sandy soil. Plant bulbs with tips level with or just under the surface of the soil.

*GLOWING CUPS of color, bright tulips stand out against ivy-covered wall. For mass effect, plant eight bulbs to 8-inch pot.*

*MORNING GLORY, sown directly in pot and later trained on stakes, forms a pillar of blue trumpet flowers, heart-shaped leaves.*

*WIRE SUPPORT is concealed by large flowers and thick foliage of 'Mme. Edouard Andre' clematis. Use pebble mulch to keep roots cool.*

## TUBBED VINES FOR VERTICAL COLOR

Container vines are indispensable on a patio or other paved surface where you can't plant directly in the soil. The climbers can be trained up a post, or a trellis can be sunk into the container.

Given a little extra attention, almost any vine can be confined — at least for a while — in a container. The extra care includes added watering and diligent nipping back and training during growth season. Usually, the slower growing vines such as ivy, annuals that do not have heavy root systems, and light, delicate kinds will perform best. Most do well in a basic potting mix. Keep an eye on root development. When it is time to repot, a take-apart tub is a blessing when you are wrestling with an overgrown vine that is anchored not only to the ground through the drain holes but also to the trellis or posts. See page 14. The container on page 32 is handy for many vines.

Here are a dozen vines that can be grown successfully in tubs and pots:

**BLACK-EYED SUSAN VINE** (*Thunbergia alata*) • Flaring inch-wide tubes of orange, yellow, or white with purple centers cover this vine, which is planted annually. Vine grows rapidly in sun and needs tying to stake at intervals. Feed monthly with complete fertilizer.

**CANARY BIRD FLOWER** (*Tropaeolum peregrinum*)• Unusual yellow flowers perch like small canary birds among rich green leaves from July until first frost. Plant seeds in light shade annually in spring. Given some support for its twining stalks, it will reach 10 or more feet and cover quickly. See page 74.

**CLEMATIS** • The deciduous, large flowered clematis hybrids that bloom in late spring or summer are best adapted to containers and are easy to train on wire or wooden frames. Use deep containers, cover the root ball with 2 inches of soil mix. When planting, put in support — stake or open wire frame. Apply a mulch to keep roots cool. Needs constant moisture and monthly feeding during growth. Bloom appears usually on new wood; cut back in late fall and move tub out of sight. Try *C. lawsoniana* 'Henryi' (8-inch flowers).

**CUP-AND-SAUCER-VINE** (*Cobaea scandens*) • Sun-loving, with bell-shaped flowers turning from green to rosy purple, the perennial vine rapidly grows to 25 feet. Plant seeds in the permanent container or start early indoors in small pots for later transplanting. Notch seeds and barely cover with soil mix. Keep moist.

**FATSHEDERA lizei** • An evergreen vine, shrubby like fatsia and climbing like ivy, the plant is heavy and needs sturdy support. If it gets out of hand, cut almost to the crown; it will regrow quickly. Likes partial shade, wind protection, and plenty of water. A good indoor-outdoor plant.

**IVY** *(Hedera)* • Widely planted, ivy is evergreen, neat, uniform, and dependable. Leaf size varies according to kind. The miniature-leafed types are best for formal training on wire forms in pots (see below) or as ground covers for large tubbed trees. Grow in sun or part shade (needs shade in hot interior areas).

**JASMINE** • Most jasmines should be planted where their fragrance can be enjoyed. All grow well in a basic mix, in sun or part shade. Pinch frequently to keep growth under control. Suggested for containers: angelwing jasmine *(Jasminum nitidum)* with pinwheel flowers, Arabian jasmine *(J. sambac),* Hawaii's pikake flower, and star jasmine *(Trachelospermum jasminoides*—not a true jasmine) with waxy, starry flowers.

**MOONFLOWER** *(Calonyction aculeatum)* • Fast-growing to 20 feet, useful for portable summer shade. The fragrant white flowers open at night. Effective in a container with morning glory. Start annually from seeds, which first should be soaked in water for two or three days.

**MORNING GLORY** • Funnel-shaped blooms are blue, white, red, or lavender, but 'Heavenly Blue' is the traditional favorite. After frosts, sow seeds of morning glory directly in the container as they do not transplant well. Provide a trellis or stake. Water moderately and do not fertilize, except in the case of Japanese Imperial morning glory, which needs rich soil and regular feeding.

**SCARLET KADSURA** *(Kadsura japonica)* • Grow kadsura for its red autumn leaves and bright winter berries. Twining, evergreen perennial, it grows fast to 15 feet and is best trained around a sturdy support. Give it full sun except in hottest climates. In spring, prune to thin and shape.

**SCARLET RUNNER BEAN** • Use this showy, twining vine for quick portable shade in new gardens. Following the red flowers are dark green bean pods which are edible and tasty when young. Plant seed in spring and give full sun.

**SWEET PEA** • A box or tub of sweet peas is a practical way for apartment or mobile home dwellers to enjoy this old favorite. Sweet peas are fragrant and excellent for cut flowers. One part peat to two parts soil is a good mix. Plant directly in container or transplant from pots or bands. Water regularly to keep vines vigorous.

*SCARLET KADSURA vine thrives on sunny patio. Fast growing, this 3-year-old vine was started from a cutting; staked and pruned.*

*TWIN IVY SENTINELS in soy tubs flank wrought iron garden stile. Ivy is trained on wires attached to inside rim of tub and center stake.*

*PLANT THREE 'White Cascade' petunias in a 9-inch hanging pot. Arching branches will be covered with large blooms into autumn.*

*VERSATILE TRAILING LOTUS is a handsome display on sunny deck railing; equally effective hanging from patio overhang. Red summer bloom.*

## HANGING BASKETS FOR EYE-LEVEL ATTRACTION

Daily watering during summer is essential for most hanging plants since they are exposed on all sides to air and wind which cause both the root ball and the top of the plant to dry out. Some kinds, such as tuberous begonias and fuchsias, may take two waterings on very hot days.

Hangers need a fast draining basic mix and three or four feedings with complete fertilizer during the growing season. See pages 8, 11 for kinds of hanging containers you can use.

Listed below are some favorite hanging plants:

**ASPARAGUS SPRENGERI** • Billowy needlelike foliage and seasonal red berries make this popular for hanging containers, indoors and out. Takes sun or part shade; best with ample watering.

**BEGONIA, TUBEROUS** *(B. tuberhybrida)* • Variety 'Pendula' with cascading sprays of vivid or pastel-colored flowers is spectacular in part shade. See page 52.

**CAMPANULA** • Trailing campanulas are excellent for bloom in late summer, fall. Vinelike stems of *C. isophylla,* blue, star-shaped flowers, trail to 2 feet; *C. i.* 'Alba,' white flowers, blooms most profusely. *C. fragilis,* trailing 12 to 16-inch stems, blue flowers with white centers, is choice but less readily available. Need filtered shade. Divide every 3-4 years in the fall.

**DONKEY TAIL SEDUM** *(Sedum morganianum)* • Overlapped succulent leaves the size of hound's teeth closely pack the pliant branches, giving the effect of burro tails. Keep this unique plant out of wind and traffic and the tails will cascade to 6 feet, draping over the container's side. It needs part shade, plenty of water, and liquid fertilizer 2-3 times a year. If you use small plants, put three to a pot to make it fill out fast. Leaves can be rooted for new plants.

**FUCHSIA** • Pendulous, freely branching varieties make splendid container plants to hang from tree branches, under house eaves, or shady patio overhangs. See page 45.

**GERANIUM, IVY** *(Pelargonium peltatum)* • Effective in a group of pots for massed color, branches trail 2-3 feet; ivy-like, glossy leaves and blooms in pink, white, rose, red, or lavender. Needs sun to develop flower color. Also good for hangers are peppermint geranium, some fancy-leafed varieties of common geranium, and a few kinds of Martha Washington geranium.

**IVY** *(Hedera)* • Many miniature-leafed forms are useful all year for their pretty all-green (or green and white) foliage. 'Hahn's Self Branching', dense light green leaves, is popular and readily available. All ivies do best in part shade. See page 55.

**LOBELIA, Trailing** • Plant several alone or in a pot with white campanula in filtered sun. See Lobelia, page 49.

**LOTUS BERTHELOTII** • Striking in earth-colored pots. The graceful stems are thickly covered with silvery foliage; narrow red blooms in mid-summer. Cut back occasionally to induce bushiness. Sun, part shade.

**PETUNIA, Cascade series** • Superior large flowers cover arching branches summer into fall. Use three plants to a 9-inch pot. 'White Cascade,' 'Pink Cascade,' and 'Red Cascade' are excellent. Protect from hot afternoon sun.

*FLUFFY PINK flowers of* Sedum sieboldii *appear in late summer. Decorative leaves turn red as weather grows colder in fall.*

## SUCCULENTS AND CACTI — DEPENDABLE AND GOOD LOOKING

Succulents and cacti are nearly perfect container plants — easy to plant, easy to grow, good looking all year, and long lived. Many kinds can be grown both indoors and outdoors.

A sandy soil mix (page 20) and perfect drainage are required by succulents and cacti. Even in summer many get by with a weekly watering. In cool weather water just enough to keep plants from shriveling. Most kinds like full sun, except on extremely hot days when they should be moved to filtered shade. One light feeding at potting time may be enough for succulents, but cacti need a monthly feeding in spring, summer. Most kinds grow easily from divisions or stem or leaf cuttings; many can be grown from seed.

### Succulents

Out of a tremendous number of different kinds of succulents, we list some favored for their foliage, flowers, or form.

**AEONIUM** • Extremely decorative, best along the coast or coast-influenced areas; tender to frost. Some varieties have reddish tinged leaves; others have tall clusters of yellow flowers; others form cushions of bright green leaves.

**AGAVE ATTENUATA** • An imposing container plant, the spineless leaves are 2½ feet long. The 5-foot wide clump bears greenish-yellow flowers on arching spikes, often soaring to 12 feet. Protect from frost and hot sun.

*UNIQUE DONKEY TAIL sedum has pliant branches that drape down over container's edge. Will cascade 6 feet in a protected location.*

*SUCCULENT COLLECTION in strawberry jar is topped with crown of* Dudleya brittonii. *Jar pockets hold sedum, crassula, and haworthia.*

*FURRY LEAVES of kalanchoe are triangular and silvery. A good indoor-outdoor plant, it is dramatic when night-lighted.*

**ALOE** • Showy and easy to grow in frost-free areas, there is a kind of aloe to bloom every month of the year. Ranging from 6-inch miniatures to 18-foot trees, they form clumps of fleshy, pointed leaves and clusters of red, orange, or yellow flowers.

**CRASSULA** • Jade plant *(C. argentea)* will stay small in a small container. Even little plants have stout trunks and limbs like dwarf trees. *C. falcata* reaches 4 feet when full-size and has dense clusters of scarlet blooms late in summer. The upright form of *C. tetragona* suggests a miniature pine tree; widely used in dish gardens or children's projects. Most crassulas can be held in the same pot for years. See page 94.

**DUDLEYA** • Striking in appearance, with rosettes of fleshy leaves covered with a heavy coat of chalky powder. The stem gradually lengthens into a stout trunk.

**ECHEVERIA** • Handsome, fleshy-leafed, flowering rosettes. Hen and chicks *(E. elegans)* has tight grayish white rosettes and pink and yellow flowers in spring. *E. setosa* has 4-inch-wide, dark green rosettes, covered with white stiff hairs; flowers are red.

**HAWORTHIA** • All are excellent pot plants which do best in part shade. Some resemble small aloes, others make little towers of neatly stacked, fleshy leaves.

**KALANCHOE beharensis** • The crimped, triangular leaves of the silvery felt plant are densely furry. Safe outdoors in mild climates with overhead protection. A good indoor-outdoor subject; it is dramatic with night lighting.

**OSCULARIA** • Foot-tall plants with trailing branches carrying thick, blue-green leaves and half-inch fragrant flowers. Good in hanging pots.

**SEDUM** • The larger kinds, such as *S. oxypetalum* and *S. spectabile,* are attractive alone in pots. The lower, creeping types combine well with some of the larger succulents. Donkey tail sedum and *S. sieboldii* (see page 57) are unusual hangers.

**SEMPERVIVUM TECTORUM** • Hen and chickens have rosettes with reddish brown tipped, bristle-pointed leaves.

**Cacti**

The following cacti adapt especially well to container living:

**CHRISTMAS CACTUS** *(Schlumbergera bridgesii)* • Drooping, spineless branches carry dozens of rosy 3-inch flowers at Christmas time. Pot in rich, porous soil with plenty of leaf mold and sand. Water frequently and feed with liquid fertilizer as often as every 7 to 10 days.

**CRAB CACTUS** *(Schlumbergera truncata)* • The jointed branches have two large teeth at end of the last joint. Flowers, white through red and orange, bloom in winter, early spring. For care, see Christmas cactus above.

**PERUVIAN OLD MAN CACTUS** *(Espostoa lanata)* • Slow-growing columnar cactus with thorns concealed in long white hair that covers the plant. Pink blooms in spring. Protect from frosts.

**SEA URCHIN CACTUS, EASTER LILY CACTUS** *(Echinopsis)* • Easy to grow, showy big flowers bloom freely in summer if given frequent feeding, fast-draining soil. Use as a houseplant; provide plenty of light. In mild climates it can be grown outdoors.

## THE DISTINCTIVE SPECIALTIES

A number of plants, because their culture is in some way exacting — or at least different from other plants — fall into a unique group referred to here as specialties. Due to their growth habits, the use you will make of them, or the care you must take with them, they require a measure of specialization on your part.

### Bamboo

Bamboo is invaluable for Oriental effects and its airy foliage makes attractive tubbed sun screens and living walls. It may be pruned and thinned to your particular liking and it is one of the few plants that continues to do well even when a little rootbound. However, you will find it unusually difficult to remove bamboo from the tub if it is left in too long. Replant every two or three years before roots have become hard and matted. See page 35 for repotting a bamboo.

These giant grasses usually require sun or at least part sun, but need heat protection when the weather becomes really hot. To keep container-grown bamboo lush and green, water and feed with complete fertilizer.

Some bamboos are ideal occupants of containers where their spreading roots can be controlled. But other bamboos are just too big and overpowering for tub culture. The kinds listed below have proved especially adapted to containers:

**BLACK BAMBOO** *(Phyllostachys nigra)* • Stems vary from pure black to olive-dotted black. Needs afternoon shade in hot areas. Grows to 4-8 feet. See page 75.

**CHINESE GODDESS BAMBOO** *(Bambusa multiplex riviereorum)* • Graceful, ½-inch-wide stems grow to 4-6 feet and carry small leaves in ferny sprays.

**GOLDEN BAMBOO** *(Phyllostachys aurea)* • Dense foliage on 6-10 foot high, thick stems; needs frequent watering to keep it attractive. Excellent in tubs.

**PALMATE BAMBOO** *(Sasa palmata)* • Handsome in large tubs and boxes, its broad leaves (to 15 inches long by 4 inches wide) spread fingerlike from stems. Will reach 4 to 5 feet in height.

**PHYLLOSTACHYS VIRIDIS** • Curving, tall stems with ferny growth at base make it an excellent plant for a narrow space. Reaches 15 to 20 feet.

### Bonsai

Basically, almost any kind of woody plant can be made into an attractive bonsai. Of course some plants are difficult to dwarf, others just don't like to spend the rest of their days dwelling in a pot. (See page 38 for soil mixes and care of bonsai, also the *Sunset* book, *Bonsai: Culture and Care of Miniature Trees.)* The following list includes some of the favorites of bonsai growers:

*TRIANGULAR BOXES are planted with golden bamboo which repeats pattern of reed screen. Keep open, delicate by cutting out extra stems.*

*GOLDEN BAMBOO fills this big 18-inch box, forming a thick screen and emphasizing the usefulness of the airy baffle behind it.*

*FLOWERING QUINCE blooms on twisted branches in spring before leaves appear. Can be propagated from cuttings, seedlings, by layering.*

**AZALEA, Kurume** • Small leaves are very dense, flowers profuse on compact, mounding plants.

**CAMELLIA sasanqua** • The bushy or spreading habits may be easily controlled by pruning. Numerous autumn and winter blooms.

**COTONEASTER** *(C. dammeri)* • Prune to enhance the twisted, prostrate branch habits. White flowers followed by red berries.

**FALSE CYPRESS, dwarf forms** *(Chamaecyparis)* • Some of these evergreens are compact little trees, others have curving or twisted branches.

**GINKGO biloba** • Graceful deciduous tree with airy, fan-shaped leaves that turn buttery yellow in fall.

**JUNIPER, Sargent** *(Juniperus chinensis sargentii)* • A classic bonsai plant valued for its picturesque form, gray-green foliage. Other prostrate kinds are also adapted to bonsai.

**MAPLE** • Trident maple *(Acer beurgerianum)* has round crown of glossy leaves that turn red, gold in fall. The Japanese maple *(A. palmatum)* and its varieties have year-around beauty. See page 42.

**PINE** • Lacebark pine *(Pinus bungeana)* has flaking gray bark that reveals creamy branches and trunk. Japanese black pine *(P. thunbergiana)*, hardy and handsome, can be pruned into various shapes.

**POMEGRANATE, DWARF** *(Punica granatum* 'Nana')  • Small red fruits follow orange-red blooms on this dense little shrub when it is only a foot tall.

**QUINCE, FLOWERING** *(Chaenomeles)* • 'Contorta' is a good choice as its twisted branches adapt easily to wiring and training into interesting shapes. White to pink flowers bloom early before leaves unfold.

**ZELKOVA serrata** • Attractive elm-like leaves turn yellow to dark red in fall.

*NEARLY FORTY years old, Japanese maple is planted in blue glazed bonsai pot. Also well suited to pot culture is laceleaf Japanese maple.*

*YOUNG DEODAR CEDAR, in early stages of bonsai training, has pale green lichen anchored on top of moss with a hairpin.*

## Ferns

Ferns are grown for their foliage — lush green, usually finely-cut fronds. Moisture loving, they need a rich soil mix and shade. Ferns with pendant or trailing stems, such as hare's foot, usually are planted in wire baskets lined with sphagnum moss. Most tree ferns are tender to frost and suffer in hot, drying winds. During growing season feed frequently and lightly with an organic fertilizer — fish emulsion is good. Peat moss mulch helps hold in the moisture.

**BIRD'S NEST FERN** (*Asplenium nidus*) • A clump of long, undivided fronds, this glossy fern can be brought outdoors onto the patio in summer.

**FIVE-FINGER FERN** (*Adiantum pedatum*) • Filmy fronds are arranged in fingerlike fashion. Grows to 3 feet.

**MAIDENHAIR FERN** (*Adiantum*) • Fronds are finely cut, dark stems are thin and wiry. Damaged by frosts, but comes back in spring. Look out for slugs, snails.

**ROUNDLEAF FERN** (*Pellaea rotundifolia*) • A small fern that is good for viewing up close because of its pretty, nearly round leaves on 1-foot fronds.

**SQUIRREL'S FOOT FERN** (*Davallia trichomanoides*) • Best as a hanging basket plant, this fern has lacy fronds curving downward; furry rhizomes (like squirrel's feet) creep over soil surface and container.

**SWORD FERN** (*Nephrolepis*) • Tough and easy to grow, sword ferns have bright green, upright fronds.

**TREE FERNS** • Dramatic tree ferns need no help from other plants to be effective. Tasmanian tree fern (*Dicksonia antarctica*) is the hardiest fern where frosts are prevalent. See page 6.

Other useful ferns for containers, indoors and out, are deer fern, lace fern, and lady fern.

*FRONDS of squirrel's foot fern cover the hanging basket. Light brown furry "feet" emerge from under fronds. House plant except in summer.*

*DEER TONGUE FERN* (Blechnum spicant) *resembles sword fern, but is more upright and stiff. Contrasts well with violets, woodland plants.*

*BIRD'S NEST FERN is unusual accent on a terrace in summer. Open clump of broad, glossy green fronds often reaches four feet in length.*

*HANGING HERBS are handy for the cook. Terra cotta pot holds cascading silver thyme, chives in bloom, and winter savory.*

*FRENCH CASSEROLE contains seven herbs growing in 3-inch pots: dwarf lavender, marjoram, thyme, rosemary, sage, peppermint, and winter savory.*

## Herbs and Vegetables

A selection of herbs in a hanging pot by the kitchen door is a convenience to any cook and a tub full of lettuce plants or a basket cascading with tiny tomatoes can bring some of the fun of growing vegetables to gardeners with limited space and even to some apartment dwellers.

**HERBS** • Long wooden boxes are attractive for herbs. For plants of varying growth habits or watering needs, divide boxes into sections or plant individually in pots. A large strawberry jar has many planting pockets for different kinds of herbs. Use in basic soil mix.

Leafy herbs are ready to be dried when flower buds begin to form. Dry until crumbly and store in airtight jars.

**Chives** • Pretty grassy clump that needs partial shade in hot areas. Rich soil, ample moisture. Feed after cutting. Divide every 3 years. Use for onion-flavor in soups, salads, gravies.

**Mint** • Spreads rapidly and must be controlled. Orange, golden apple, peppermint, and spearmint are available for cold drinks, tea, or lamb. Mint is used also in jelly and for garnishing. Replant every 3 years.

**Oregano** • Leaves, fresh or dried, are one of the distinct flavors of Mexican and Italian cooking. Grow in sun. Water moderately. Trim to prevent flowering; replant every 3 years.

**Parsley** • Fernlike foliage can be used year-around. Seeds are slow sprouting. Parsley should be planted annually. Needs sun or light shade, ample watering.

**Rosemary** • Plant the prostrate form of common rosemary in full sun, slightly gravelly soil. Do not overfeed or overwater. Use leaves to season meats and soups.

**Sage** • Narrow gray leaves on bushes to 2 feet; spikes of fragrant violet flowers. Takes full sun. Divide every 3-4 years. Use leaves fresh or dried. Feed plant after cutting.

**Summer Savory** • Sow seeds in place in full sun and rich soil. Long, narrow, aromatic leaves can be used either fresh or dry as a mild seasoning.

**Sweet Marjoram** • Keep this favorite herb quite moist and in full sun. A good indoor herb in cold areas.

**Tarragon** • Shiny, dark green leaves on slowly spreading branches; dies to ground each winter. Cut sprigs in June for seasoning vinegar. Use leaves fresh or dried for fish, vegetables, eggs. Divide every 3 or 4 years.

**Thyme** • Aromatic common thyme grows best in porous soil that is fairly dry. Keep plants bushy by nipping back tips. Grow from summer cuttings.

Don't hesitate to try any of the other herbs that appeal to you, including the richly fragrant ones such as lemon verbena and lavender.

BOXFUL OF HERBS is located near kitchen door, includes pots of parsley, chives, mint. Herbs can also be planted in divided sections of box.

BIG SQUASH grows in rich soil in washtub. Sow several seeds 1 to 1½ inches deep in a big container and water lavishly.

**VEGETABLES** • Many vegetables are as attractive as they are edible when you single them out for display in a container. These especially may surprise you:

**Cucumbers** • It takes a lot of water to grow cucumbers (also squash, pumpkins, and melons). Fill a big container to the brim at least once a day. The soil should be a rich mixture of loam, sand, leaf mold and commercial fertilizer; or compost.

**Eggplant** • The big purple fruit is spectacular. Set out plants in early spring, feeding every 6 weeks with commercial fertilizer. Soil should be rich and porous.

**Lettuce** • A large tub or box planted with loose leaf lettuce offers an attractive way to grow a supply of tender salad greens. Sow seed or set out transplants in loose, fairly rich soil in early spring. Provide frequent, light feeding, regular watering, and part shade (in warmer areas during the hottest part of the day).

**Kale** • The curly kales, especially bright-leafed flowering kale, are decorative container plants. Harvest outside leaves for cooking.

**Peppers, Green and Red** • Handsome, bushy pot plants. Water thoroughly but not too frequently during growth. Feed once or twice with commercial fertilizer after blooms set.

**Rhubarb** • Big leaves and red-tinted stalks are showy. Plant roots in late winter, early spring in deep, rich soil mix. Water freely as leaves form. Allow two seasons of growth before harvesting. Protect from snails.

**Squash** • The broad, squat bushes of summer squash are best adapted to containers. Choose from 'Early Summer Crookneck', 'Early White Bush', or 'Caserta' (zucchini). Culture same as for cucumbers.

RED VEINS of ornamental cabbage intensify in cold weather. Seeds available from specialty seed companies; plants from some nurseries.

*OVERHEAD CHERRY TOMATO crop is decorative, nutritious, unusual. Branches grow horizontally, later hang down with weight of full crop.*

*FIRM SOIL around one strong tomato plant in 12-inch pot, leaving 1½-inch rim free for water—cherry tomatoes take a lot.*

**Swiss Chard** • An easy plant to grow from seeds; plant in early spring in a sunny place. After 2 months you should be able to cut outside leaves as needed for meals.

**Tomato** • Most tomato varieties, if staked and supported, can be raised in big, deep containers. However, a dwarf tomato or a gay cherry tomato are better adapted to pot or basket culture. Dwarf 'Tiny Tim' and 'Atom' bear tasty, tiny fruits on upright plants. Place one plant in a 6-inch pot, two or three to a 10-inch pot.

A cascading cherry tomato is a patio conversation piece. Buy established plants, placing one husky plant in a 12-inch hanging pot, leaving a 1½-inch rim free for water. Provide a porous, rich soil and water daily in hot weather. Feed twice at 3-week intervals, starting 3 weeks after potting. Dust occasionally with fungicide-insecticide before fruit sets.

## Plants in small pools

When you think of pool plants, water lilies usually pop first into mind; but specialists sell many other aquatic plants that send up leaves or blooms above the water surface. Although you can plant them directly in soil on the bottom of the pool, it is easier to care for the plants and keep the pool clean if you use boxes or other containers. Glass, plastic, and wood are all satisfactory, but avoid using redwood as it discolors the water.

Water plants are easy to grow but have one definite requirement — they must have full, or nearly full, sun. A recommended soil mix consists of 4 parts loam mixed with 1 part commercial slow-acting complete fertilizer (look for a nitrogen content of 3 to 5 per cent).

Listed below are the smaller water plants that are best adapted to the limited depth of a small pool. If your pond is large there usually are taller or huskier kinds of the same plants available. At nurseries specializing in pool plants you will find many additional choices. Ideas for pools are shown on page 84.

**HORSETAIL** (*Equisetum hyemale*) • Rushlike, 4-foot hollow stems with distinct joints. Vigorous growth. Sink pot halfway up in water.

**LOTUS** (*Nelumbo*) • Huge leaves and fragrant 4 to 10-inch-wide summer flowers rise above water level. Ornamental woody fruits with perforations like a salt shaker are useful in dried arrangements. Plant in spring in 12-inch-deep container; place so soil surface is 8 to 12 inches under water. In winter, protect from freezing by covering pool or storing roots. Lotus roots don't like corners, but do well in a *round* pot or tub.

**JAPANESE IRIS** (*Iris kaempferi*) • Graceful, sword-shaped leaves and velvety summer blooms enhance a pool. Set rhizomes 2 inches deep in potting mix and plunge pot halfway to rim in pond. Not adapted to hot, dry areas.

**PAPYRUS, DWARF** *(Cyperus haspan)* • Long thin leaves in filmy green clusters top 18-inch stems, give a pond an Oriental look.

**UMBRELLA PLANT** *(Cyperus alternifolius)* • Spreading leaves like the ribs of an umbrella top 2 to 4-foot stems. *C. a.* 'Nanus' is a dwarf form. In cold areas, keep over winter as house plant.

**WATER LILY** • Rounded leaves, deeply notched at the base, float on the surface. Showy flowers float or stand above water on stiff stalks. Two types: hardy lilies, which stay in pool all winter; tropical lilies, which must be stored and replanted in all but mildest climates.

For small pools, choose dwarf kinds of hardy or tropical lilies; *Pygmae helvola* and *Laydekeri* are among the smallest and best blooming. Generally, each small lily needs about 4 square feet of water surface. In spring, set rhizomes or tubers just beneath the soil surface in boxes about 8 inches deep. The dwarf kinds will grow with 4 inches of water over the root crown, but do better with at least 8 inches.

**WATER SNOWFLAKE** *(Nymphoides indicum)* • Lacelike, inch-wide flowers with petals resembling snowflakes rise a few inches above the water surface. Leaves somewhat like those of water lilies. Grow in a container filled with 6 inches of potting mix. Set box so that 6 inches of water is above the soil surface.

Other interesting water plants are: pickerel plant (with blue bloom spikes), arrowhead, cattail, and water hyacinth (will grow in semi-shade).

*HORSETAIL CLUMP graces one end of small garden pool. Vigorous grower, horsetail is planted in partially submerged pot hidden by rocks.*

*WATER HYACINTHS flourish in a precision molded concrete bowl. The bowl was cast in a Chinese cooking wok. Designed by Mrs. Clark H. Gates.*

*DISCARDED LAUNDRY TUB becomes a miniature garden pool afloat with dwarf water lilies. Tub edge is hidden with planting of baby's tears.*

*ENTRYWAY is ideal location for dramatic thread-leaf false aralia, which reaches a height of 5 feet in two to five years.*

*'DOLLY DIMPLE', miniature African violet, fits into a tea cup. Neat mound of heart-shaped foliage is topped with dainty light blue flowers.*

## HOUSE PLANTS

The pleasure of sharing a home with favorite plants is especially appealing to some gardeners, whose involvement may range from near-neglect of some tough plants like *sansevieria* to fastidious attention to others like African violets and orchids. General instructions on potting and care of house plants are on page 36.

The plants named below are among the most popular and reliable of the hundreds grown indoors.

**AFRICAN VIOLET** • Colorful clusters of flowers stand above a neat low mound of fuzzy, heart-shaped leaves. Best in east window with suffused morning sun, high humidity. A good potting mix is 3 parts leaf mold, 1 part loam, 1 part builders' sand, and a small amount of bonemeal. Bloom is best when roots are crowded. Use slightly warm water for watering and avoid splashing on leaves or crown.

**AGLAONEMA** • Leaves deep green, veins pale green; flowers resemble small white callas. Plant grows 2 feet high. One of the best for poorly lighted situations.

**ARALIA, THREADLEAF FALSE** *(Dizygotheca elegantissima)* • Leaves on young plants are narrow, divided into lacy, fanlike clusters atop stems. As plant matures leaves become coarser. Give ample light, feed monthly, and spray for pests.

**ASPARAGUS SPRENGERI** • Long, drooping stems clustered with bright green needlelike leaves. A good indoor-outdoor plant. Popular for hanging baskets.

**CHAMAEDOREA ELEGANS** • Often called parlor palm, it is the best palm for indoors. Tolerates crowding and poor light; grows slowly to 3 or 4 feet.

**COFFEE** *(Coffea arabica)* • Tall, upright shrub clothed with shiny leaves. Small white fragrant blooms followed by red fruits each containing two seeds—coffee beans. Use a porous, acid mix; place in well-lit spot.

**FIDDLELEAF FIG** *(Ficus lyrata)* • Dramatic, huge, fiddle-shaped leaves. Needs a large planter and a situation where it can grow tall.

**GERANIUM** *(Pelargonium)* • Most plants in this large group have showy flowers and pretty foliage — fancy-leafed, trailing, or scented. Allow geraniums to become nearly dry between waterings; provide full light each day. They do well when somewhat potbound.

**IVY** *(Hedera)* • Many variations of this vine — large or small, green or variegated, heart-shaped or deep-lobed leaves. Excellent for small pots or big indoor planters, depending on kind.

**ORCHID** • Special treatment is required by orchids. Generally, they need a planting mix of osmunda fiber, hapuu (tree fern bark), or a commercial orchid mix. Most require a high light intensity (behind sheer curtains in an east window is good) and high humidity.

While moisture is important, overwatering will rot orchids. When the soil looks dry and the pot feels light when lifted, the plant needs water. Repotting is needed every two years. The best time is when the new roots start to grow, shortly after flowering.

Orchids are either epiphytic (grow natively in tree branches and derive nutrients from air and moisture) or terrestrial (grow natively in moist, humus-rich soil).

This list includes those most favored for bloom and the easiest to grow as house plants:

**Cattleya** • Best known, one to four blooms per stem.

**Cypripedium** • Elegant, glossy lady's slipper orchid.

**Epidendrum** • Easiest to grow, bears clusters of miniature orchids.

**Oncidium** • Long arching sprays of blossoms make excellent cut flowers.

**Odontoglossum** • Includes the striped tiger orchid and fragrant lily-of-the-valley orchid.

**PHILODENDRON** • Tough, durable house plants known for attractive, leathery leaves in many sizes and shapes. Usually vining, plant needs support, good light, and ample water. Common *P. oxycardium* will grow in water.

**SANSEVIERIA** • Thick, banded leaves that radiate up from base. Leaves of *S.* 'Hahnii' are blunt triangles; *S. trifasciata* has stiff sword leaves 1 to 4 feet tall. Grows in little light, seldom needs repotting, and withstands dry air and spasmodic watering.

**SENTRY PALM** (*Howeia belmoreana*) • Slow-growing, feathery palm is ideal house plant. It withstands some neglect, drafts, and dust.

**SPLIT-LEAF PHILODENDRON** (*Monstera deliciosa*) • Becomes very large with huge, dark green leaves, deeply cut and perforated with holes. Its long-term indoor use requires a large area and a strong support.

*GRACEFUL OLD-TIMER, airy asparagus fern spills sprays of foliage over sides of 16-inch pot held high on a curved wrought iron stand.*

*A DOZEN chamaedorea palms clustered in small 12-inch white porcelain bowl. Excellent indoor palms, these grew only eight inches in five years.*

*PHILODENDRON AND IVY are features of indoor planter with metal lining and watertight drawer to catch seepage.*

# WHERE TO PUT THEM
# AND HOW TO USE THEM

Quick effects • Portable shade • Screening • How to disguise walls, beautify buildings
Desert planting • Decks, roof gardens • Small pools • Apartment, mobile
home patio planting • Plants for foliage, fruit, bloom, and berries
Displaying specimens • Entries • Movable fragrance
Night lighting • Gift plants, children's projects

Frequently, after you have chosen and potted a plant that is especially appealing, you are at a loss as to where to put it. Unless you have many container plants with a definite plan for rotating them for spring bloom, autumn color, and other effects, it is a good idea to think about placement before you select the container and the plant.

## USE PLANTS TO SOLVE PROBLEMS — OR JUST FOR PLEASURE

Container plants can play a variety of roles. They can be utilitarian stagehands on the garden scene — forming barriers to keep intruders from special spots, screening an area from breezes, or filtering the sunshine. They also can disguise the unattractive lines of a structure or, conversely, emphasize and enhance a good structural design.

Plants in containers give a new garden a lived-in look. Window boxes and tubbed plants become the "gardens" of apartment and mobile home dwellers.

*RAINY DAY SCENE vividly demonstrates garden value of a large number of container plants. Consider how gloomy this mid-winter scene would be without the variety of numerous potted plants.*

From an esthetic standpoint, patios, decks, and roof gardens are not only improved by the presence of container plants, they sometimes are entirely dependent upon them.

On the whole, most container plants are best in a starring role — as plants that give you *pleasure*. There is no other type of gardening that is so personal, that so involves your responsibility to the plant, or that even borders on sentimentality in the way that raising your choices in containers does. Therefore, container plantings deserve to be placed where they can be seen, where your glance will fall upon them several times a day.

Give your container plants a chance to perform for you if they have a special feature. If you have a tubbed daphne it should be placed near an entry in the late winter so that you can enjoy the delicious fragrance every time you open the door. It would be a shame to exile it to a rain-sodden garden where you easily could miss most of its bloom and fragrance season.

Consider also making your collections — bonsai, succulents, geraniums — a part of your landscaping scene with special areas where they can be seen and enjoyed. Or, fill boxes with dusty miller, nicotiana, or white alyssum to softly illuminate a patio on a dark day or a moonlit night.

In this chapter you will find numerous landscaping and interior situations that either are enhanced by or dependent upon the presence of container plants. Ideas for garden pools, children's projects, and plants that can be decorated also are included.

# Plants that Solve Problems

A plant in a container often adds the extra element that solves an interior or landscaping problem. Tubbed plants can soften the harsh lines of a new wall, dress up an entry, or hide a garbage can. Potted trees pro- vide shade or screen off an area for privacy. All but the biggest containers can be moved about to where they are needed at the moment. The following pages show ways to put container plants to work.

## QUICK EFFECTS IN A NEW GARDEN

*TEMPORARILY GROUP plants selected for later planting in new garden. Sink cans in peat-filled boxes outside windows or at entry.*

*NEW, SMALL PATIO enlivened by use of potted dwarf marigolds in boxes attached to fence, geraniums at the edge of the brick patio.*

*ONE JUMBO-SIZED concrete container massed with soft pink petunias makes a spectacular showing. For repeat bloom, cut back after flowering.*

*NEW HOME ENTRY is enhanced for the time being with a collection of potted geraniums, blooming in shades of pink, white, and bright strawberry.*

## SHADE THAT IS MOVABLE

*MORE THAN just decorative, the handsome loquat serves as a portable shade tree, or as a screen for blocking the wind or an unwanted view.*

*NEATLY PRUNED as round-headed standard, Ficus macrophylla in large twin pots creates shade on oceanside terrace but does not interrupt view.*

*SHADE COMES FAST with ornamental fig — it grows rapidly to 6 feet and the leaves are enormous. Feed and water frequently.*

*PLASTIC SCREEN secured in long planter brimming with colorful summer annuals is one way to block the hot afternoon sun. Move box with rollers.*

*REDWOOD PLANT BOXES filled with evergreens serve as buffers to cars in this parking area next to a garage. Design by Chandler Fairbanks.*

*GOOD IDEA for decreasing patio traffic comes from Marbella, Spain. Large pots make portable barriers to protect* alfresco *diners.*

*WAIST-HIGH RETAINING WALL forms a trough to hold numerous pots of junipers and Southern Indica azaleas which perform beautifully in sun.*

*ROW OF PITTOSPORUM in 30-inch square redwood boxes gives importance to the entry area and also helps to separate it from adjacent driveway.*

*HANGING CONTAINERS with green ivy provide some privacy from neighbors who look down onto deck; useful for interrupting hot late afternoon sun.*

*RAISED ABOVE usual level of the garden, a deck often has a privacy problem. A fence of bamboo in boxes makes a good screen.*

*COLUMNAR EVERGREENS grouped closely give an attractive look year around, provide privacy and a background for pots of summer flowers.*

*OUTDOOR SHOWER is just about a must when you live near the beach. This one is partly curtained by a lacy podocarpus in a handsome, ornate pot.*

THREE PLANTS of canary bird flower trained on wires against side wall of garage. Seeds of vine can be sown right in the container in spring.

SPIRALING AND GRACEFUL, this living room stairway design is repeated in the towering feathery fronds of a tubbed palm.

LONG WALL on street side of house seemed blank after remodeling. Redwood boxes with Hollywood junipers dress up the scene.

*FEATHERY LEAVES of* Chamaedorea seifrizii *reach upward toward skylight. The tall cluster of palms is impressive in entry hall.*

*YOUNG PYRACANTHA adds color to light-toned masonry wall. Support for fast-growing branches is made of 2 by 4's bolted to wall.*

*BLACK BAMBOO divides and delicately screens the living room from the entry hall. Rotate two tubs of bamboo frequently between indoors, out.*

*SMALL HEXAGONAL beds are the only garden in otherwise completely paved area. Wind resistant succulents in pots are sunk in gravel in bed.*

*STRIKING FOLIAGE of brassaia dominates the sky-lit planter separating the living and dining area. Design by Douglas Rucker.*

*SERIES OF POCKETS in deeply recessed windows hold plantings of large-leafed philodendron, which is effective also from indoors.*

*BRICK-RIMMED planting pocket breaks up wide expanse of entry court and serves as a display spot for ponderosa pine and tamarix juniper.*

*OFTEN A WALL exposes too much brick, stone, or wood and seems monotonous. Lavender starflower (Grewia caffra) relieves expanse.*

*STAR JASMINE planted in Mexican strawberry jar traces a delicate pattern against the soft rosy orange burnt adobe wall of entry court.*

*VIVID COLOR of bougainvillea spills over sides of planter wall. Bougainvillea also makes a blazing show trained up against a wall.*

*TAPERED GLAZED POTS, 16 inches in diameter, rest in holes in concrete shelf built into wall. Colorful planting relieves both long wall and paved area.*

*SWORDLIKE LEAVES of yucca planted in full sun, signal entry to adobe brick home. Cast concrete container designed by John Svenson.*

*SIMPLE CONTAINER planted with hopbush (Dodonaea viscosa) adds to dramatic landscape. Water cascades from pipe in natural crack in rock.*

*TOLERANCE to low winter temperatures makes Mediterranean fan palm a good choice for colder sections of desert.*

*LIKE WINGS of a giant bird,* ramada *of reinforced concrete provides shelter from desert heat. The dramatic, ascending form of large container plant echoes the columnar saguaros in the desert beyond. Other heat-tolerant potted plants decorate the paved area.*

*PINEAPPLE GUAVA, planted in terra cotta pot made in Mexico, accents one side of adobe brick terrace. Guava receives full sun.*

*OPEN DESERT is only minutes away, but there is little to suggest an arid climate in this lush garden. Hibiscus in pot is featured.*

# Gardening in Small Spaces

When a garden is limited in size that small space becomes more important than ever, as its good looks and usefulness are dependent upon the plant chosen and the way it is displayed. Pot gardening on a limited scale is pictured on the following pages, showing areas such as roof gardens, decks, apartment and mobile home patios that are restricted to plants that are grown in containers.

## DECKS DEPEND ON CONTAINERS

*GENEROUS SIZE planter holds graceful, mounding evergreen that dresses up deck and is transition to garden scene beyond.*

*LOVELY TILE DECK under an ancient tree is an excellent stage on which to display prize bonsai and other container plants.*

*VERSATILE PLANTER on deck is an entire garden in itself. Back part is platform for pot plants. Foreground is small pool lined with fiberglass.*

*EMPTY THE POOL and put in a number of container plants. Summer color of petunias contrasts with greenery of tubbed plants on platform.*

THIS DECK, although it is large in size, is entirely dependent upon plants in containers to repeat the feeling of the planting beyond the bench and guard rail. Dark green conifers in soy tubs fit naturally into the lakeside scene and geraniums in foreground give cheery color.

TRIO OF PLUMP pots with sunny petunias makes this deck inviting. Cluster of tubbed plants thrives in background in filtered shade from lath overhang.

ONE UNUSUAL container plant is often all a deck needs for a focal point. Fifteen-year-old pindo palm is somewhat dwarfed in original pot.

*BANKED ON DECK, benches and steps, container plants give an ever-changing effect. Owner of lagoonside home is expert container gardener who works with 200 clay pots, 150 redwood boxes. Deck has places for all phases of pot gardening, from those out of bloom to those ready for display.*

*GOOD IDEA for watering a number of pot plants on a high deck. Hose is pulled through hole in floor with gasoline station type hose rollers.*

*POTTED PLANTS are clustered in informal groups on bedroom deck and enhance an unusual elevated sunning platform.*

## GARDENING ON ROOFTOPS

*BLUE AND WHITE urns add elegant touch to roof ledge. Junipers grow in boxes inside urns, which rest on thick wooden stands.*

*ALL ELEMENTS of regular patio are present in this city rooftop garden. Trees for shade, bright potted perennials, small pool are features.*

*ROOFTOP DECK over a garage features sections of decking and Mexican pebbles placed in checker-board pattern—striking spots to display succulents and bamboo; planter boxes for interesting, shallow rooted plants. A trailing plant in a hanging pot is suspended from the airy overhang.*

*SQUARE POOL at the end of a garden bench features Japanese iris and water lilies. Acanthus (lower right) and rhododendrons banked behind.*

*THREE-BY-FIVE pool is just the right size for two 'White Star' water lilies. Clump of horsetail grows in corner in submerged pot.*

*DRAMATICALLY TERRACED, this shallow garden pool has no planting other than Cyperus alternifolia, which is controlled in thick ring containers.*

*HALF BARREL POOL is a charming place to try water plants; the right size to accommodate one tropical water lily 'White Star' set in its own pot.*

*SALAD MAKINGS right outside the door! Lettuce, chard, and parsley look refreshing in white glazed pots. Cut off leaves as needed.*

*WOODLAND GARDEN, complete in a portable redwood box, features ferns and shrubs, but plant groups could represent desert or seaside.*

*FOR MOVABLE DISPLAY, attach casters to low box and fill with damp peat moss to prevent rapid drying out of collection of small plants.*

*EFFECTIVE WAY to use a small square provided in apartment garden. Curb off section with bricks, sink a pot of bird of paradise, plant succulents.*

# Plants for Pleasure

Most of the plants we put into containers are there just because we like them: for unusual foliage, a pleasing fragrance, a dramatic form when night-lighted. On the following pages you will find suggestions for places for your favorites and ways that you can use them for greater enjoyment.

## FOLIAGE TO VIEW UP CLOSE

*CHARMING DWARF PINE* (Pinus densiflora *'Umbraculifera') in blue ceramic pot is displayed beside a small pool on a brick terrace.*

*JAPANESE MAPLE in white pottery container has been pruned lightly to reveal trunk, branch pattern. Enjoyed all year at entryway.*

*DRAMATIC CYCAD is placed on patio table where its feathery leaves can be viewed up close. Cycads need a partially shaded location.*

*SUPERB STANDARD, four-year-old 'Southgate' fuchsia bears dozens of dancing pink and white blossoms. 'Swingtime' is also good.*

*SPRING SCENE on* Sunset's *patio shows citrus tree in large Spanish pot at left; boxes of tulips, poppies, violas, and alyssum on ledge.*

*PORTABLE PEACH tree is 'Bonanza'. Its natural dwarf habit keeps tree within container bounds and fruit within reach.*

*TEN STRAWBERRY plants in a two-foot square plant box should yield berries in mid-spring. Traditional strawberry jar could be used.*

## SPECIAL PLANTS ON DISPLAY

*EXTRA WIDE SILL in kitchen between window and screen creates a protected pocket for a collection of favorite small plants.*

*ORNATE URN with white oleander, trailing lotus sits atop pile. Planter adds color, dresses up dock, and discourages seagulls from perch.*

*COLLECTION OF BONSAI, expertly trained by John Naka, range in age from ten years (second from right) to two hundred (third from right). Displayed on redwood benches with ample room to show off each specimen; background is reed matting.*

'SHOWCASE' GARDEN *is seen through bedroom window. Tiny enclosed garden room is open at top. Azaleas, jade plant, wisteria in containers.*

GRACEFUL, PENDULOUS *flower clusters droop from wisteria branches in spring. Pleasing branch pattern is displayed beautifully.*

OLD COPPER KETTLE *displays large aspidistra as patio feature. Old-fashioned favorite, aspidistra is hardy, nearly indestructible.*

PLEASANT CORNER *of a graveled terrace where the end of a bench is used to display an attractive jade plant as well as stoneware bowls, tiles.*

*ARRIVING OR LEAVING, you are met with container plants at this entry. Indoor plants thrive in light location by window grille.*

*FORMAL TOPIARY tree is three wire mesh globes welded to pipe in box. Ivy cuttings set from outside into moss-lined, soil-filled globes.*

*ANGULAR AND PICTURESQUE, evergreen is a product of careful, controlled pruning. Tall, smooth pottery urn complements plant in sunny entry patio.*

*'MAGIC MOUND', bright yellow miniature chrys-anthemum, stationed in twin pots beside entry; resemble living pincushions dotted with color.*

*YOUNG YUCCA in pot on seat wall and loquat in tub at right of door. Plants repeat desert growth beyond. Protect loquat from reflected heat.*

*PAIR OF TEN-year-old rhododendrons in brassbound redwood tubs frame the doorway with rose lilac blossoms in prominent clusters. Iris in clay pots on step add to the lush springtime appearance in a patio bordered with plants.*

*POWERFULLY FRAGRANT* Rhododendron fragrantissimum *is enjoyed near entry during spring bloom. Slightly tender, protect during severe cold.*

*CLUSTER BIG LILIES around a patio post and delight in the lovely fragrance. After bloom, reduce watering and repot in autumn.*

*DELICIOUSLY SCENTED, Hawaii's frangipani (Plumeria) is ornamental in bloom, starkly dramatic when it loses leaves in spring.*

*GARDENIA NEEDS summer heat and filtered shade to produce fragrant blossoms and glossy foliage. Keep soil moist.*

*MUGHO PINE, floodlighted from behind container, appears as a magnificent burst of light. Dense growth blocks glare even when viewed close up.*

*EFFECTIVELY LIGHTED, aralia on patio seems a part of both indoors and outdoors. Enhanced at Christmas by glowing paper star.*

*LARGE LEAVES of lighted plant in pocket outside window reflect floodlighting from below, give soft glow inside room.*

*ENTRY PLANT beside doll house door is crassula. Its small scale makes it a believable pine tree in miniature setting. Sugar bowl container.*

*IVY PYRAMID decorated with metallic paper stars. Six rooted cuttings trained on six bamboo stakes tied together at top.*

*DWARF BOXWOOD cuttings set closely in 5-inch, glazed white Italian pots. Little plants are decorated with gold balls and candles.*

*CUT OR BREAK stem from mature jade plant, place in small container with sedum at base. Prop up bent stem with twig. Add gift card.*

# INDEX

**Boldface numbers refer to photographs**

## PHOTOGRAPH CREDITS

**William Aplin:** 35 (bottom left), 45 (right), 47 (right), 50 (left), 52, 54 (bottom), 65 (top), 71 (bottom left), 72 (bottom left), 73 (bottom right), 77 (top left, bottom left), 78 (top right), 81 (bottom right), 84 (bottom left), 86 (bottom right), 87 (bottom left), 88 (bottom), 91 (top left, bottom), 93 (right). **Aplin-Dudley Studios:** 10 (right), 39, 45 (left), 67 (left, bottom right). **Jeremiah O. Bragstad:** 90 (top right). **Morley Baer:** 63 (top left), 70 (top right). **Ernest Braun:** 6 (right), 12 (top, lower left), 32, 49 (left), 51, 55 (right), 59 (right), 67 (top), 73 (top right), 75 (right), 77 (top right), 78 (left), 79 (top), 82 (top), 83 (top), 89 (bottom left), 91 (top right). **Guy Burgess:** 71 (top left). **Clyde Childress:** 44 (right), 93 (top left). **Glenn M. Christiansen:** 7, 9 (bottom), 13 (top), 15 (bottom), 16 (top right), 17 (left), 18, 28, 30 (top), 31, 37, 43, 47 (left), 57 (left), 66 (top), 70 (bottom right), 84 (right), 87 (top left), 90 (top, top right), 93 (bottom left). **Robert Cox:** 8 (bottom), 11 (top left), 13 (bottom), 33, 59 (left), 76 (bottom left), 87 (bottom right). **Richard Dawson:** 4, 6 (left), 10 (left), 11 (bottom), 12 (lower right), 15 (top), 16 (top left), 44 (left), 53 (bottom), 78 (bottom), 79 (left), 85 (top), 87 (top right). **Richard Fish:** 75 (top), 80 (top right), 81 (top, left), 82 (bottom right), 83 (bottom), 84 (top left). **Alan W. Farrant:** 25 (bottom left). **Phil Fein:** 74 (left). **Frank L. Gaynor:** 79 (bottom left). **Jeannette Grossman:** 11 (top right), 46 (left), 50 (right), 72 (top left). **Walter Houk:** 80 (bottom left). **Helen Hull:** 92 (bottom left). **Art Hupy:** 63 (top right). **Tatsuo Ishimoto:** 89 (top left). **Dorothy Krell:** 35 (right). **Roy Krell:** 58 (right), 68, 72 (top right), 76 (top right), 77 (bottom right), 88 (top right), 89 (bottom right), 92 (bottom right). **Samson B. Knoll:** 92 (top right). **Ellsworth Marugg:** 17 (center left). **Jack McDowell:** 38, 60 (bottom right). **Proctor Mellquist:** 49 (right). **Herbert V. Mitchell:** 21. **Don Normark:** 34 (bottom left), 36, 61 (top), 85 (top right), 86 (left), 93 (top left). **Phil Palmer:** 80 (top left). **Ron Partridge:** 56 (right). **Charles R. Pearson:** 71 (bottom right). **Martha Rosman:** 74 (top, bottom), 89 (top right). **Blair Stapp:** 14 (top). **Darrow M. Watt:** 9 (top), 14 (bottom), 16 (bottom), 17 (right), 25 (bottom right), 26, 27, 29, 30 (bottom), 48, 51 (top), 53 (top), 54 (top), 56 (left), 58 (left), 60 (top, bottom left), 61 (bottom right), 62 (top), 64, 65 (bottom left), 66 (bottom), 70 (top left, bottom left), 76 (bottom right), 86 (top), 94. **R. Wenkam:** 82 (bottom left), 88 (top left). **A. W. Williams:** 57 (right). **George Woo:** 55 (left).

**Cover photograph: Robert Cox.**